Beaconsfield Golf Club

1902 – 2002

Gordon Tuck

Grant Books, Worcestershire 2002

ISBN 0 907186 47 5

Published in a limited edition
of 975 copies

Typeset in 11 on 13 point New Baskerville
and printed in Great Britain by
Hughes & Company
Kempsey, Worcestershire, England
Bound by Cedric Chivers Ltd., Bristol

Published for Beaconsfield Golf Club by
Grant Books
The Coach House, Cutnall Green,
Droitwich, Worcestershire WR9 0PQ
www.grantbooks.co.uk

Contents

Acknowledgements

Beaconsfield and Beaurepaire by Robert L. Baird & Gisèle Hall

Beaconsfield and District Historical Society

Berks, Bucks & Oxon Union of Golf Clubs

Colt & Co. by Fred Hawtree

Cynthia Tipson, Professional Golfers' Association

Golf Weekly 2002 incorporating Golf Illustrated

Major J. Mills & Colin Wharton, Defence School of Languages, Wilton Park

Imagemaker, Amersham

Denis Pannett for permission to reproduce his painting of the clubhouse

The Bucks Free Press incorporating The South Bucks Free Press

The Final Links by Dennis Edward and Ron Pigram

The History of Wilton Park by S. J. Anglim

David Stirk for a photograph from Golf – The History of An Obsession

The British Golf Museum

Val Doonican for his sketches

Preface

IN APRIL 1902 the Sino-Russian Treaty over Manchuria was concluded, a massive blaze destroyed a large area of the Barbican in the City of London, a state of emergency was declared in Ireland, twenty people died when a stand collapsed at the Ibrox Park football stadium in Glasgow and the Wilton Park Golf Club on the Du Pre Estate at Beaconsfield (population 1,524) was instituted. The course extended to nine holes. Among the trophies for which members competed in those early days was the Sir John Aird Challenge Cup – a name familiar to present day members of The Beaconsfield Golf Club.

A new course designed by Harry Shapland Colt upon the commission of Lt. Colonel William Baring Du Pre was opened in 1914 and it is clear that the new Club was a continuation of that founded in 1902. The names of members featured in local newspaper reports of the annual prize giving of the original Club appear again in the minute books and records of the Beaconsfield Golf Club Limited, incorporated in December 1913.

The story of those early days, the transition into the present-day members' Club and of the developments since the incorporation in 1948 of the current company (originally called Wilton Park Golf Club Limited) set out in this book makes a fascinating read. However, the book is clearly much more than that. It is the product of a very considerable quantity of painstaking research and a work of considerable scholarship upon which its author, Gordon Tuck, and those who have assisted him in those researches are deserving of our congratulations and grateful thanks.

The publication of this splendid book is surely a most fitting way to mark the hundredth anniversary of the foundation of the Club.

Roger Connor

His Honour Judge Roger Connor,
President, October 2002

Foreword

SEVERAL YEARS ago, a former president wrote to the then secretary of the Club to ask if it was possible to establish the significant anniversaries of the club and, in particular, when its centenary should be celebrated. Would it, he asked, be a hundred years after the Beaconsfield Golf Club was opened in 1914, a hundred years after the members purchased the Club in 1948, a hundred years after the Wilton Park Golf Club was instituted in 1902 or some other date? Strange as it may seem, it was not possible at that time to answer the question with any certainty and it was not until the year of the Millennium – though that year in itself has no specific relevance – that a definitive answer could be given. The answer was "In 2002".

It so happened that it was about that same time that I had expressed an interest in putting together something about the history of the Club – though not, I must add, with any thought of writing a book.

My interest in the history of the Club began, I suppose, when, as a member of the Royal Army Educational Corps, I was posted for a short while in 1955 to the Army School of Education at Wilton Park. Among my memories of that time are those of playing croquet on the extensive lawn at the rear of the White House which was then the Officers Mess, but which in former times had been the Du Pre family home. That initial interest received a further stimulus when, after leaving the army and returning to the law, I settled in Beaconsfield and became a member of the Golf Club in 1968. It was from then on that I gradually began to understand and then to appreciate the long connection between the club, the Du Pre family and the Wilton Park estate.

And so it was that, when the date of the Club's centenary had been established and it was thought that the publication of a book for members on the history of the Club would be an appropriate project for the occasion, I rashly and immodestly agreed to undertake the task of writing one in time for it to be published at the end of the centenary year. In retrospect, it is clear that I had not fully appreciated the demands that such a time-scale would impose or just how much material there was to be uncovered.

Nevertheless, with considerable help and encouragement along the way, I have completed the task, albeit inadequately, and it has been an experience that has added greatly to my own understanding and appreciation of what it means to be a member of Beaconsfield Golf Club. History, they say, is a great teacher and for my part I have been absorbed by the learning process. I have had the enormous pleasure of being a member of this traditional golf club for some thirty-four years and now I have had the added privilege of piecing together the jigsaw of its history. I am most grateful for both experiences and I can only hope that this book will contribute, if only in some small measure, to the reader's own appreciation and enjoyment of their membership of the club.

The task of producing the book within the available time would not have been possible without the assistance of many fellow members of the Club, of members of the Artisans' club and of various other people. Unfortunately, they are too numerous to mention by name and, in any case, my memory would surely fail me in trying to remember all of them. Nevertheless, I extend my sincere thanks to each and every one of them for their considerable help and advice.

There are a few people, however, whom it would be unpardonable of me not to mention by name.

His Honour John Slack, himself a member since 1970, is someone to whom I and the whole Club owe a very great debt of gratitude for his meticulous researches that made it possible for the Club to establish the necessary continuity between Beaconsfield Golf Club and the original Wilton Park Golf Club so as to give the former a foundation date of 1902. Moreover, without his considerable endeavours, our knowledge of some aspects of the very early years could have remained scant indeed.

Vesey Raffety is a name that occurs frequently throughout the book, for he was a man who contributed greatly to the Club's affairs as a member, as a captain and as a President. Even though he is no longer with us, my thanks to him must be recorded for his delightful, ten page account of the history of the Club up to 1951 on which I have taken the liberty to draw. This account is referred to in the book as "the Raffety account". I would ask his widow, who now lives in Brighton, to accept my thanks on his behalf.

My thanks also go to Wendy Gardiner, that stalwart organiser of the Beaconsfield Salvers, for allowing me to draw on her short history of the Ladies' section.

Val Doonican, who has been a member of the Club now for twenty-five years, is a man of many talents as well as golfing ability, and I am most grateful to him for the various sketches of the clubhouse and the course which he has kindly drawn especially for inclusion in the book and which now grace several of its pages.

Many of the photographs of the centenary and other recent events at the Club have been taken by two of its relatively new members, Terry Sellick and Suzanne Karchargis. I am enormously grateful to them not just for several of their photographs that appear in the book, but also for using their professional skill and digital camera equipment to enhance, as if by magic, some of the old photographs and other material that as a result, I have been able to include.

I am greatly indebted to Gisèle Hall, a member of the Beaconsfield Golf Club in Canada, for information about the history of that club and for the delightful book that she co-authored on the history of *Beaconsfield and Beaurepaire*. My thanks also go to Joyce Cooper, a member of Burnham Beeches Golf Club, for information and memorabilia of the time that her husband, Jack, was steward at Beaconsfield and likewise to Jimmy Hume, the professional at Gullane, and his wife for the help that they have given me.

Mary Stevens and Derek Randall have very kindly devoted a great deal of time to reading the typescript of most of the book and I am grateful to them for their helpful suggestions and for their encouraging support.

Last, but by no means least, I must express my sincere thanks to my wife, Barbara, for tolerating so patiently the long periods of domestic isolation that she has inevitably had to endure. Her forbearance has indeed been sorely tested over the last two years, but it has not been found wanting. Nevertheless, I must now make amends.

Gordon Tuck

Chapter One

Wilton Park and the Du Pre Family

THE HISTORY of Beaconsfield Golf Club is rooted in the history of the Wilton Park estate and the Du Pre family who owned it for almost two centuries. It is, therefore, most appropriate to begin the story of the Club with a brief account of the estate and the family.

The Wilton Park Estate

Although Roman times are often the starting point of the history of important places, in the case of Wilton Park it is not necessary to go that far back. And yet, if members were to do so, they would probably encounter a cohort of Roman soldiers marching steadfastly across what is now the practice putting green, then along the 17th fairway to the 16th green and onwards to the south-west, heading for Silchester on the Roman military road from St Albans. A straight line drawn from one to the other passes through Beaconsfield.† Such knowledge, while probably of little comfort, may be of passing interest to the golfer who is wont to slice his ball at the 17th hole – for just beyond the first bunker and a few yards inside the "Out of Bounds" fence on the right hand side lies, slightly raised and discernible, what is undoubtedly a small section of that very Roman road.

In their book *Roman Roads in the South-East Midlands* published in 1964, the authors, "The Viatores", trace the route of the St Albans – Silchester road in detail and on page 145 write:

> The line continues south-west through the north-western gully at the junction between Longbottom Lane and the road to Seer Green, and up the field to the other side of the gully without surface indications. It goes under the Beaconsfield Golf Club, across the links and through Walk Wood to Wilton Park …

Walk Wood is the name of the wood that lies to the right of the 17th hole and if, without unduly delaying play, the golfer were to look along the line of this section of track, he would find that it points directly to the clubhouse.

†*Essay on the History of Beaconsfield* by members of Beaconsfield and District Historical Society.

1

Nor is that stretch of Roman road the oldest relic of past ages to be found on the Wilton Park estate for about a hundred yards from the 3rd tee in the woods to the right – probably far beyond where even the most extreme of slices could penetrate – lies a very well preserved, conical shaped Bronze Age bowl barrow. Minor undulations still mark the position of the ditch from which the material for the mound was excavated. The presence of the "Mound" is marked on Ordnance Survey maps and it has been scheduled by English Heritage as an Ancient National Monument.

Foxglove on the Roman Road
by Val Doonican

The old town of Beaconsfield developed around the important cross-roads of the London-Oxford road running east-west and the north-south road running from what was then the county town of Buckingham to the Royal Borough of Windsor. A crossroads situated as it was at a comfortable day's coach ride from four such important towns could not fail to become an important staging post, and this explains the considerable number of hostelries for weary travellers and horses that have been and, in much smaller measure, still are a feature of the four "Ends" of the Old Town.

In addition, giving importance and character to the town as it developed around this crossroads, were the great estates of Beaconsfield such as Hall Barn, Butler's Court and Wilton Park.

The original boundaries of the Wilton Park estate are not now known and they certainly would have changed during its long history, but the heart of the estate is the area of land enclosed by the Oxford Road (A 40) to the south, the Amersham Road to the west, Longbottom Lane to the north and Potkiln Lane to the east. The estate did, however, include land on which much of the new town was built and also land to the north of Longbottom Lane. It was a large part of that land at the east end of Longbottom Lane, including Dean Farm, that Colonel Du Pre sold to the Committee of Friends in April 1918 and on which Jordans village was then developed.

At the time of its first known recorded mention in 1184, "Bekenesfeld" formed part of the Burnham Hundreds and the land which was later to emerge as the Wilton Park estate belonged to an Anglo-Norman family known as the "de Burnhams". By 1265, the estate had passed to Richard, Earl of Cornwall, who presented it to the Abbey of Burnham as part of its initial endowment. The monks then leased the estate to a succession of families including the "de Wheltons" from whom, through variations such as "Whiltones", the estate eventually derived the name by which it is still known.

2

Wilton Park House in the nineteenth century

The Du Pre Family

The Du Pres were French Huguenots who, with others of their faith, fled from France after the St Bartholomews Day massacre in 1572 and in the decades that followed. Many of them, including the Du Pres, made their way to London and, in due course, established successful businesses in that part of London which, for obvious reasons, became known as Petty France.

It is not known for certain when the Du Pre family first appeared on the Wilton Park scene. One account reports that it was in 1773 when the family took a lease of the estate for one year and then returned in 1779 as owners after Josias Du Pre had bought the estate from the Capel family. Another account puts the purchase date as a year later. Yet a third account, and the one mentioned in the Raffety account,† has it that Josias Du Pre bought the estate from the Basill family as early as 1760, which was some six years before he married Rebecca, a sister of the Earl of Caledon, at the parish church in Beaconsfield. Wherever the truth lies, the Wilton Park estate was to remain within the Du Pre family for most of the next two centuries.

There is also uncertainty as to when the principal house on the estate was actually built. Some have it that the main part was built in the early eighteenth century during the time of the Basill family's occupation and that the two single storey north and south wings were added towards the end of

†As explained in the Foreword

the century. Others, while acknowledging that there was a house of substance at Wilton Park when the Basills owned the estate, believe that the White House was in fact built from the considerable fortune that Josias Du Pre had amassed from his service with the East India Company and, subsequently, while he was Governor of Madras. According to this version, Josias died in 1780 before the house was completed and it was left to be finished by his widow.

Built of Portland stone, the White House, as it came to be known, was a most imposing building whose obvious symmetry greatly added to the splendour of its Palladian style. And in its heyday, the furnishings and its noted works of fine art would have ensured that its interior was no less imposing. It was in this very same White House that, well over a century later, annual prize-givings of the Wilton Park Golf Club were to be held by invitation of Sir John Aird who was the tenant of Wilton Park at the time.

On the death of Josias Du Pre in 1780, the title to the 350 acre estate passed to his son, James, who died in 1870 at the age of ninety-two. James' son, Caledon George Du Pre, who succeeded to the estate, served as Member of Parliament for Buckinghamshire for thirty-two years and died without issue in 1886. It is probably at this point in the long history of Wilton Park and the Du Pre family that the history of Beaconsfield Golf Club can really be said to have begun, for it was then that the estate passed to Caledon's great-nephew, William Baring Du Pre.

The Du Pre Family Coat of Arms

On 3rd April 1826, a coat of arms, registered as "Grant 36/3" in the records of the College of Arms, was granted "to James Du Pre of Wilton Park in Buckinghamshire and Portland Place in Middlesex, High Sheriff of the former county, and to other descendants of his father the late Josias Du Pre, sometime Governor of Madras".

In his petition for the grant, James Du Pre stated that "…his family was formerly seated in France from whence his Ancestors emigrated and settled in this Country …" and that "… on examination of the Archives of the College of Arms he is informed that the Armorial Bearings borne by his Ancestors have not been duly recorded …" and that, therefore, "… he was making application for the grant of a coat of arms as similar as possible to the one used by his family previously …"

4

Immigrant families, even if entitled to the same or a similar coat of arms in their original country, were not and still are not automatically entitled to a grant of arms in this country, but it was not uncommon for petitioners in this country to make reference to arms that had been granted elsewhere. Several Huguenot families who came to this country, and who claimed use of a coat of arms in France, applied for grants of arms *de novo* in England soon after they arrived, but the Du Pres were by no means alone in not applying for a grant of arms for several generations after their first immigration.

The coat of arms granted in 1826 consisted, as was customary, of a shield surmounted by a crest. The heraldic description of the shield itself is that it is "Azure, a Chevron Or, between in chief two Mullets and in base a Lion passant Argent issuant from the centre chief a Pile Or". More simply stated it is blue with a gold upward-pointing chevron with two silver five-pointed stars above it and below a silver lion passant, that is to say, a lion walking on all fours to the left.

The crest itself consists of a silver lion rampant with its right hind foot resting on a red fleur-de-lys; or, in the more sophisticated language of heraldry, "a lion rampant Argent resting its dexter hind paw on a fleur-de-lys Gules".

The bar immediately beneath the crest (or, as it has somewhat disrespectfully been called, "the horizontal barber's pole") and on which the fleur-de-lys and the lion's left hind paw rest, marks out the design as a proper heraldic crest as opposed to a free-standing, quasi-heraldic device, and it represents a side-on view of a circlet of twisted cloth. The colours of this twisted cloth are alternately gold and blue. The symbolism in a family's coat of arms is not always easy to discover and often remains a private matter for the grantee. So far as concerns the Du Pre coat of arms, nothing is known about its symbolism and, while it is probable that the fleur-de-lys symbolises France from where the family had immigrated, it is somewhat less certain whether the lions, rampant or passant, symbolise England, the family's adopted country.

The crest is joined to the shield by a helmet embellished by what appear to be oak leaves. This embellishment, which in heraldry is technically called "mantling", is a stylised representation of ragged cloth flowing from the circlet of twisted cloth upon which the lion's paw and the fleur-de-lys stand.

The motto associated with the coat of arms is old French and, somewhat freely translated, means "He who would lose faith, will lose honour" – a sentiment that must surely reflect the commitment of this Huguenot family to its faith.

A stonemason's reproduction of the Du Pre coat of arms can be seen on the memorial tablet to Lt. Colonel Du Pre and his first wife that was erected on the north wall of Beaconsfield parish church by their daughters.

The Club's Crest

In recognition of its connections with the Du Pre family, the Club adopted the crest part of the Du Pre coat of arms. It has not been possible to establish when that occurred, but it is of comparatively recent times. There is certainly no evidence that the crest was used by the Club while Colonel Du Pre was alive or, indeed, for some years after the Club became a members' club in 1948. The first reference to its use by the Club is contained in a Board minute of June 1955. Over the previous four years the Board had been discussing the question of a club tie and had asked the secretary to trace any previous colours that the club had used. He duly reported back that the club colours were black, silver and gold – although it was not said nor is it known on what he based that assertion. At the June meeting, the Board considered various tie samples that had been submitted by Messrs T. M. Lewin & Sons of London and these incorporated the "motif of the lion taken from the Du Pre coat of arms

– for which permission had been given". The tie with that motif on a "medium blue background"† was duly chosen and forty-eight such ties were ordered that same evening for sale to members at 22s.6d. Unfortunately, it is not known what colours were used in the depiction of the lion on the sample tie or on the new club flag incorporating that logo which Vesey Raffety presented to the Club when he retired as captain later that year. The lion crest is engraved on the Lidgley Shield that was presented in 1960 and it probably came into general use at the club at about that time. Certainly the Club's List of Fixtures and Members for 1966 and 1967 and much of the stationery in use at that time display the crest.†

However, when the lion crest was first used by the Club, it did not include the bar of twisted cloth on which the lion's left hind paw and the fleur-de-lys rest; that was a later addition. In the 1970s, the crest was enclosed in two concentric circles. The colours used in the Club's reproductions of the crest have also varied from time to time, probably for technical reasons having to do with the material on which they were being reproduced.

The club logo as used at various times

---

† At much the same time, the Beaconsfield Cricket Club adopted the lion motif with a dark green background. Colonel Du Pre was its President from 1925 to 1946.

Lt. Colonel William Baring Du Pre

William Baring Du Pre was born on 5th April 1875 and was only eleven when his great-uncle died. That meant that he was not able to succeed to his inheritance at Wilton Park for another ten years, by which time he had completed his education at Winchester and Sandhurst and had been com-missioned into the King's Royal Rifle Corps.

He came to Beaconsfield to take up his inheritance on 7th May 1896 and, according to contemporary accounts, the day was indeed a day that the townsfolk would long remember.

A wonderfully descriptive account of this festive occasion appeared in the *South Bucks Free Press* (as it then was) the following day:

Lt. Colonel William Baring Du Pre

The circumstances attending the celebration of the coming of age of Mr. W. Baring Du Pre and his succession to the Wilton Park estates at Beaconsfield, yesterday afternoon, will long be remembered in the history of the town … The weather could not have been more favourable for the occasion, and on all hands the inhabitants entered into the rejoicings with the greatest enthusiasm….the residences on both sides of the High Street were embellished with flags and other adornments, while the roadway was extensively lined with streamers and flags. In addition, there was an arch of evergreen erected at the Wycombe end of the town and this bore the word "Welcome" in conspicuous letters.

In the Broadway there was a canopy of streamers attached to Venetian masts, while at the entrance to Wilton Park an arch of greenery was surmounted by the motto "Welcome Home". In front of the steps leading to the mansion another arch of evergreen, with flags depending, was erected, and the motto upon this was "Health and Prosperity". Mr. Du Pre arrived from London at the Wooburn Green station at a quarter past two, and accompanied by his mother, he was at once driven to Beaconsfield. Upon entering the town the carriage was met by a number of sons of tenants of the Wilton Park estates, who took the horses out, and, substituting ropes for the traces, pulled the vehicle to a point nearly opposite the Saracen's Head Hotel. Here, the carriage was surrounded by a numerous gathering of the inhabitants, who heartily cheered Mr. Du Pre.

The bells of the Parish Church were also ringing at the time, while cannon were fired in Wilton Park in honour of the event.

Subsequently a series of rural sports were indulged in in the grounds, and at night there was a display of fireworks, a huge bonfire being also lighted.

A similarly colourful account was written in the Parish Diary by the Reverend G. A. Cooke, who became Rector of St Mary and All Saints in Beaconsfield later that year. He concluded his account with the words: "Everything went off very successfully. The weather was bright and warm. An event of this kind does a great deal to cultivate good relations between landlords and tenants, rich and poor."

William Du Pre was at this time a second lieutenant in the Second Battalion, King's Royal Rifle Corps and, after a brief settling in at Wilton Park, he returned to his battalion in Malta and then sailed with it to Cape Town. The following years saw him in and out of the army several times serving variously for short periods with the Imperial Yeomanry, the Leicestershire Yeomanry and also with the Leicestershire Battery of the Royal Horse Artillery. Hart's *Army List* for 1919 records him as having retired from the army at the end of the First World War and becoming a Lt. Colonel in the Imperial Yeomanry. It was during this period of his frequent absences with the army that Colonel Du Pre lived either in London or at Taplow House in Taplow and the White House was leased to various tenants. Sir John Aird, to whom reference is made in Chapter Two, was one such tenant.

In 1903, Colonel Du Pre married Miss Youri Wynyard, daughter of a naval captain. They had one son, who tragically died in his early teens, and three daughters who became Honorary Members of the club. Youri died in 1942 and three years later the Colonel married Beryl, widow of Major the Hon. Robert Dudley Ryder of the 8th Hussars.

Although he is said to have had a single figure handicap, in his younger days golf took very much of a second place to croquet as the Colonel's greatest sporting love. He was an outstanding croquet player and a leading figure in the international world of croquet, having won the world championship on numerous occasions. He was a member of the Roehampton Club (as well as the Carlton and the United Services Clubs), he captained the English croquet team for several years and toured with them in Australia. He was known to have visited France on several occasions to give croquet lessons. With such dedication to the game, it is not surprising that, at the rear of the White House, there was a large and immaculate croquet lawn which was, according to one of his daughters, her father's pride and joy. The lawn remained a feature of the extensive gardens until the house itself was demolished in 1967, but there are still a few members of the Club who, while members of the RAEC officers mess at Wilton Park, actually played croquet on this hallowed turf, though not, if they are honest, to anything like the standard of the Colonel.

For Colonel Du Pre himself, golf and croquet were not wholly different sports, for he putted croquet style. As George Greenwood, reporting in the

Daily Telegraph on 11th December 1920 on the recent match between Beaconsfield and the Stage Golfing Society, put it:

> He is a firm believer, from long and toilsome practice, of the croquet mallet style ... He is a distinguished croquet player, but was induced to adapt to the mallet style of putting upon the advice of a champion of the game. He even has a special club fashioned for the purpose. It is a concentric iron head with a perfectly upright shaft....The Colonel stands facing the hole and swings the club between his legs.[†]

The same reporter also revealed that "Colonel Du Pre plays the wrong way round; in other words he is a left-hander. He hits every drive with an unintentional pull and slice, and the effect is rather pleasing on a calm day."

His army and his sporting activities would probably have been enough for most people, but not for Colonel Du Pre. Politics were well and truly in the Du Pre family blood – his predecessors at Wilton Park had, at various times, represented several constituencies including Aylesbury, Chichester and Buckinghamshire – and it was only to be expected that at some stage Colonel Du Pre would also seek to become a Member of Parliament. His first attempt was at the General Election of 1906 when he unsuccessfully contested the Loughborough Division of Leicestershire. His political ambition was eventually achieved in 1914 when he was elected Conservative MP for the High Wycombe Division of South Buckinghamshire – a seat he was to hold until he was defeated in 1923 by the Liberal candidate. His attendance at Parliament was, of course, interrupted by the First World War during which he saw service in the Middle East with the Royal Horse Artillery (Territorial Force Reserve).

He was appointed a magistrate for Buckinghamshire and in 1911, like his great-uncle before him, Colonel Du Pre was made High Sheriff of the County.

As will be seen later, during the Second World War, Wilton Park was requisitioned by the army and from then until his death in 1946 Colonel Du Pre lived in Ascot at a house called Tetworth and never returned to live at the White House.

Such then was the background of the man who brought golf to Beaconsfield in 1902 and who, for the next forty-four years, was utterly and enthusiastically committed to making Beaconsfield one of the most prestigious golf clubs in the country.

[†]An amendment to the Rules of Golf in 1968 banned the croquet style of putting.

Chapter Two

Wilton Park Golf Club
1902 to 1914

THE TURN of the nineteenth Century saw a remarkable expansion in the popularity of golf among the great and the good generally but especially in London and the south-east. New clubs mass-produced from hickory and persimmon and imported from America together with the new imported wound rubber "Haskell" ball had added excitement to the game, while the rapid development of the railway network meant much easier access to golf courses. All this led to the staggering increase in the number of golf clubs and golfing societies in the first decade of the century from 2,300 to well over 4,000.[†]

It was in this climate of excitement and expansion that the story of golf in Beaconsfield was set to begin in 1902. At that time the population of the town was only 1,524, it was spread over some 4,500 acres and it was lit by gas provided by a private gas company whose works were on Penn Road, now Station Road, adjacent to Davenies Farm, now Davenies School. Apart from a few farms and one or two houses, there was no "New Town" for the railway had yet to be built.

Wilton Park Golf Club

The first recorded mention of Wilton Park Golf Club is the entry in the "Club Directory" section of the 1908-1909 edition (Volume XXII) of the *Golfing Annual*:

> **BEACONSFIELD – WILTON PARK GOLF CLUB**. Instituted April 1902.
> *Entrance Fee*, 21.2s.; *Annual subscription*, 21.2s.; *Number of members*, 80.
> *Hon. Secretary* – O. G. Johnston, Parkside, Beaconsfield, Bucks.
> *Green Records* – Professional 37, by R. Mackenzie; Amateur 39, by O. G. Johnston.
> The course, of nine holes, is a mile from Beaconsfield Station. Visitors, 1s. a day, 4s. a week, or 12s. a month. Sunday play without caddies.

A further entry regarding the Wilton Park Golf Club appeared in Nisbet's *Year Book* for 1914 which recorded that the Club's membership had risen to

† *Golf – The History of an Obsession* by David Stirk.

100. Most interestingly, this entry actually records the length and the bogey ("par" in today's parlance) of each of the nine holes as they were at that time:

Hole	Yardage	Bogey		Hole	Yardage	Bogey
1	340	5		6	140	3
2	375	5		7	420	5
3	413	5		8	176	4
4	311	5		9	360	5
5	250	4			2785	41

In fact, these were probably not the measurements of the original nine holes at Wilton Park because in the summer of 1908 changes had already been made. Reporting the club's annual prize-giving for that year, the *South Bucks Free Press* correspondent wrote:

> Thanks to the energy of Mr. Oliver Johnston, the Club Secretary, and his groundsmen, the competitions were held over the new course, which was in excellent condition, the links having been recently greatly improved by being altered and considerably lengthened.

The precise location of the nine hole course is unlikely now to be established with certainty. The Raffety account speaks of the clubhouse, "if as such it could be called", as being "a building nothing more than a shed at what was one of the entrances to Wilton Park at the corner of the Oxford Road and Potkiln Lane". The lodge house at this entrance to the estate can still be seen and the "shed" was probably located further along the drive from that lodge. The generally held view is that the course was located somewhere on that part of the estate bounded to the south by the Oxford Road, to the east by Potkiln Lane and to the north by the main estate driveway running from the Potkiln Lane lodge pass the White House to the lodge at London End. It may well have stretched alongside the Oxford Road as far as what is now the Pyebush roundabout but probably not much further because, by 1902, Colonel Du Pre had given Beaconsfield Cricket Club permission to use land in that area for its ground – land that it still occupies and now owns.

With few records and no photographs available, it is very difficult to imagine what life was like at the Wilton Park Golf Club. The clubhouse, being no more than a "shed", probably served as little more than a place in which players changed their shoes – in those days it was not customary to change into any other clothes in order to play golf – and it probably had little, if anything, in the way of refreshment, lounge or other clubhouse facilities. Nevertheless, something of the atmosphere of the time can be gleaned from the contemporaneous reports that appeared in the *South Bucks Free Press* of the club's annual prize-givings which took place in May or June each year from 1907 to 1912. During most of this time, Colonel Du Pre was not at Wilton Park and Sir John Aird, as tenant, was the actual occupier of the White House. The report of the 1907 prize-giving reads:

WILTON PARK GOLF CLUB
Presentation of Prizes

The Wilton Park Golf Club is fortunate in having as one of its members so generous a gentleman as Sir John Aird, Bart., who annually provides prizes for competition both by lady and gentlemen members. The contests for these were concluded on Thursday, May 30th, when prizes were presented at Wilton Park House where several of the members were assembled. Sir John Aird, after welcoming his guests on behalf of his wife and himself, called upon Mr. Johnston for a description of the competition and results. Mr. Johnston, having described the various phases of the competition, proceeded to read the results of the ladies' competition in which Miss E. C. Hill and Miss L. Ankatell secured first and second places respectively. Sir John Aird then presented Miss Hill with the first prize consisting of a handsome silver clock and a thermometer combined. The second prize, an elegant chatelaine and case, was handed to Miss Anketell. During the rounds some very exciting games were played, especially the semi-final ladies match, when a stubborn fight between Miss E. C. Hill and Miss D. Young had to be carried to the 21st hole before Miss Hill could secure a victory by one stroke.

Mr. Johnston then announced the result of the competition for the gentlemen's prizes. Mr. O. G. Johnston, the winner of the first prize, was presented with the handsome challenge cup, and Mr. H. V. Raffety with a silver cigarette case as the second prize. In this competition, there were some keenly contested matches particularly Mr. H. V. Raffety and Mr. H. J. Johnston, Mr. Raffety winning by a stroke on the last green. Mr. Raffety also beat Mr. F. H. Myers by the same margin in the semi-final.

Mr. O. G. Johnston proposed a hearty vote of thanks to Sir John Aird for the prizes and to Lady Aird for her kind hospitality. This was warmly supported by Mr. H. V. Raffety and carried unanimously.

Tea was then served in the drawing room, and Sir John placed both his house and grounds at the disposal of his guests, who thoroughly enjoyed the opportunity of admiring their surroundings. It was a great pleasure to a lover of pictures to inspect the works of art to be seen at Wilton Park House, and to have the opportunity of quietly admiring a work so famed as "The finding of Moses" (by Alma Tadema) or so fine an example of the later work of Lord Leighton as to be seen in his picture of "The Slinger".

Similar, though shorter, reports of the prize-giving occasions in subsequent years appear in the same newspaper and from these the continuing interest of Sir John Aird in the welfare of the Club is manifested not only in his inviting the Club to hold its annual prize-givings at the White House, but also in continuing to donate prizes "for the ladies and the gentlemen's competitions". Sir John's involvement in and support for golf at Beaconsfield will be remembered for as long as competition for the Sir John Aird Challenge Cup is held.

Was there a Club Professional?

It is most unlikely that there was a professional golfer attached to the Wilton Park Club at any time during its existence and certainly there is no mention of there being a professional in any of the press reports referred to above.

However, the entry for the Club in the 1908-1909 "Club Directory" does mention the professional record of 37 for the nine hole course as being held by "R. Mackenzie". Moreover, in a book published in 1911, there is a reference to the formal opening of Flackwell Heath Golf Club in the spring of 1905 and this reference records that the opening events included an exhibition match played by four "local professionals", namely: Sherlock (Oxford), Turner (Gainsborough), McKenzie (Beaconsfield) and Simpson (Maidenhead).

It is tempting to conclude, despite the different spellings of the name, that this "McKenzie" is one and the same person as the "R. Mackenzie" who held the professional record at Wilton Park and that that person was, therefore, the "local professional" at the Club at least around 1905. But it is not that simple.

The only record that the Professional Golfers' Association has of an "R. Mackenzie" or a "McKenzie" at the relevant time relates to a "Robert McKenzie" (known as "Mac") who was the professional at Stanmore Golf Club from 1909 until 1949. The *History of Stanmore Golf Club* records that, immediately before taking up his position at that club, "Mac" had been "the private professional to Lord Burnham and had helped construct a course for him that had been designed by James Braid". Since Lord Burnham's estate was then (as now) at Beaconsfield, the probability is that the "McKenzie (Beaconsfield)" who played in the exhibition match at Flackwell Heath was, so to speak, Lord Burnham's Mckenzie and was not the professional at Wilton Park even though he would seem obviously to be the same person who held the professional record for that course in 1907.

The Demise of Wilton Park Golf Club

Although there are no records or accounts of the closing of Wilton Park Golf Club, its demise is clearly linked to the opening of the new golfing facility in 1914 on another part of the Du Pre estate.

Why and when Colonel Du Pre first conceived the idea of constructing a new course and clubhouse will probably remain a mystery, but there were probably several factors. The ever increasing popularity of golf, the increasing success of the Wilton Park Club, the recognition that nine hole courses were becoming things of the past and his own growing interest and skill in the game all probably played their part in his decision. So also did the fact that competition from eighteen hole courses in the neighbourhood had been growing apace since the Wilton Park Club itself had opened in 1902; courses at Flackwell Heath (1905), Ellesborough (1906), Stoke Poges (1908), Denham (1910) and Swinley Forest (1910) had already been opened. It is not without significance that, of these courses, the last three had been designed

13

A pause in the excavation of the railway cutting near to what is now the 6th tee

by the then rising star in golf course architecture, Harry Shapland Colt, for it was to him that the Colonel turned to design his own new course.

All these may have been contributing factors, but the most significant factor that influenced the Colonel's decision to build a new course and clubhouse on a different part of his estate must have been the coming of the railway to Beaconsfield in 1906 – and, of course, the substantial compensation that he received as a result of the line going through his estate.

The Railway comes to Beaconsfield

The railway line that runs from London through Beaconsfield to Birmingham and beyond was authorised by Act of Parliament in 1899. Its construction was a joint initiative of the Great Western Railway and the Great Central Railway and was the last main railway line to be built in England. Evidence of this collaboration between the two great railway companies still exists in the form of a boundary marker post which can be seen to the right of the path leading from the Staffordshire blue brick tunnel at the end of the visitors' car park to the 11th tee. This marker post, which strangely enough is actually located on Club property, bears the inscription "Great Western & Great Central Railways".

The construction of the line through the Chilterns was particularly difficult and necessitated the building of high viaducts, the excavation of several long tunnels and cuttings and the felling of numerous mature trees in the beech woods on the Wilton Park estate. Nevertheless, the entire project, which cost an estimated £40,000 a mile, was completed according to plan on schedule and train services began on 2nd April 1906. The first ticket issued at the Beaconsfield station was to Lord Burnham.

Among the various covenants† included in the land transfer for the rail route through Wilton Park was one imposed on the railway developers that called for a station halt to be constructed adjacent to a "Golf House" that was proposed to be built at a specified place on the estate – suggesting of course that the building of a new golf club adjacent to the railway line had been in the Colonel's mind for some years before 1914. The halt was eventually constructed by GWR engineers and was opened for use on 1st January 1915 – some six months after the official opening of Beaconsfield Golf Club itself.

Initially, the halt was designated "Beaconsfield Golf Platform" (1906), then "Beaconsfield Golf Links Halt" (1915) and then "Seer Green" (1918). In 1922, the Committee agreed to the GWR's proposal to change the name to "Seer Green Halt for Beaconsfield Golf Club and Jordans", but two months later the Committee changed its mind. Sometime later during the 1920s the station nameboard was changed to read "Seer Green & Jordans – Alight here for Beaconsfield Golf Club" and it is now simply "Seer Green and Jordans".

Several of today's members may still recall playing the railway holes while being engulfed by what, to steam enthusiasts, would have been the exhilarating smoke of the likes of the *The Master Cutler, The South Yorkshireman, The Birmingham Pullman, The Belfast Boat Express* and *The Inter City.*

As for the old nine hole course, it can only be assumed that it was abandoned and, with the advent of the war in 1914, was probably turned over to agricultural use.

Beaconsfield Golf Club – the Successor to Wilton Park Golf Club

With the approach of what would have been the centenary of the Wilton Park Golf Club in 2002, the Board of the Beaconsfield Club became concerned to know whether that Club should properly be regarded as the successor to the former one at Wilton Park so as, in effect, to constitute the two of them one continuous club. The advice received from the British Golf Museum in St Andrews, the body that acts in these matters for the R&A, was that, given adequate and appropriate evidence of continuity, one club can be recognised

---

†It is said that another such covenant required at least one "up" train and one "down" train per hour to stop at that station "for the convenience of golfers" but, given later correspondence with the railway companies in question about the infrequency of stopping trains, there probably was no such covenant.

His Honour John Slack whose research into the early days uncovered valuable information and established the continuity between the two clubs

as being the direct successor of another even though they may have had different names and/or different locations.

It was in large measure through the evidence uncovered and pieced together by one of the Club's members, His Honour John Slack, that the Club was able to demonstrate the necessary degree of continuity. By correlating the names of competitors mentioned in contemporaneous local newspaper reports of the annual prize-givings at Wilton Park with names mentioned in the early minutes of the Beaconsfield Golf Club and in other source materials, John was able to establish beyond doubt that at least eleven male and two female members of the old Club became members of the new Club. These included:

Mr. H. J. Johnston who was secretary of Wilton Park Golf Club for an unknown period up to 1907 and who became a committee member (1919-1924) and captain (1925) of Beaconsfield Golf Club.

Mr. O. G. Johnston who was secretary of Wilton Park Golf Club (1907-1914) and who won the Sir John Aird Cup there in 1907, 1908 and 1909. There is a reference in the Beaconsfield Golf Club minutes to his handicap being adjusted by the Committee on 2nd April 1921. [The two Johnstons, Henry and Oliver, both resided at Parkside, London End, Beaconsfield, and are thought to have been father and son.]

Mr. F. W. & Mr. L.W. Myers who are recorded as being among the competitors for the Sir John Aird Cup in 1907 and whose handicap adjustments are recorded in the Beaconsfield Golf Club minutes for 17th July 1920.

The Rev. A. S. Commeline, who having retired as rector of the parish of Burnham in 1901 after twenty-six years in that position, was chairman of Wilton Park Golf Club and was a Beaconsfield Golf Club committee member in 1920.

Mrs. J. Bailey-Gibson, wife of a Beaconsfield solicitor who himself became a member of Beaconsfield Golf Club, was named as one of the competitors in a competition in 1911 at Wilton Park Golf Club and is recorded as having resigned from Beaconsfield Golf Club in 1921.

So far as concerned the secretaries and professionals, no evidence of continuity was found. The last secretary at Wilton Park had been Oliver

Johnston and, while it is almost certain that he joined the Beaconsfield Club when it opened, he did not take on the position of secretary with the new Club, for that position went to Captain Fleetwood Pellew, a nephew of Colonel Du Pre. As regards professionals, there probably never had been a professional at the Wilton Park Club and, in any case, the first professional at the Beaconsfield Club was J. H. Jones who came to the new club in 1914 from Bexhill Golf Club.

However, in addition to continuity of membership, continuity in the important area of club medals and trophies was also established, and the evidence for this focused on the Sir John Aird Challenge Cup.

Sir John Aird Challenge Cup

As already mentioned, Sir John Aird was one of the tenants of Wilton Park. He leased it from 1905 until 1911 and during that time he was very supportive of the Wilton Park Club. In 1906, he had presented a "handsome challenge cup" to be played for each year by the gentlemen members of the club in a knock-out competition, but that cup became the property of Oliver Johnston in 1909 when he won it for the third successive year. However, as the *South Bucks Free Press* account of the 1910 annual prize-giving reports, Sir John had "generously presented another silver challenge cup to replace the one he had presented four years ago". This is the very same cup that, except for the war years and for 1925, has been

The Sir John Aird Cup

played for annually ever since it was first presented. The names of all the winners since 1910 are engraved on the cup which also bears the following inscription:

Wilton Park Golf Club
Annual Challenge Cup
Presented by
Sir John Aird, Bart
– 1909 –

When this cup was played for just before the outbreak of the First World War in 1914 the winner was Harold Raffety, who was one of those members of Wilton Park who became a member of the new club when it was formed. It so happened that Harold's son, Vesey Raffety, who was later president of the Club from 1963 to 1969, won the cup just before the outbreak of the Second World War and Vesey was known to remark frequently that,

17

The Railway Tunnel by Val Doonican

for the sake of the nation, it was to be hoped that a Raffety would never again win the cup.

By 1939, the competition for the Sir John Aird Cup had become, as it is now, a medal as opposed to a match play competition and, in those days, it was the custom at Beaconsfield, as at most clubs, for the winner of a trophy to receive a replica – a costly custom that has now largely been discontinued. Recently, Vesey Raffety's widow has most kindly loaned to the Club the very replica of the cup that her husband received in 1939.

The Board and then the British Golf Museum accepted this evidence as establishing the continuity between the two clubs and so, since the 2001 edition, *The Golfer's Handbook* has officially listed the foundation date of the Club as being 1902.

Subsequent to these events, the file copy of a significant letter has been discovered which puts the matter beyond all doubt. The letter was written on 1st February 1920 by the then assistant secretary of the Club, George Langley-Taylor, to the Dunlop Rubber Co. Ltd. in connection with its motorists' guide to the country's golf courses and in it the secretary wrote on "Beaconsfield Golf Club" headed paper saying: "You will notice a change in the name of this Club which was Wilton Park Golf Club originally. In your next issue please omit the words 'Wilton Park'."

Chapter Three

Beaconsfield Golf Club Ltd
1913 to 1918 – The Beginning

Incorporation of the New Club

IT WAS ON Christmas Eve 1913 that a company bearing the name "Beaconsfield Golf Club Limited" was incorporated as a private limited company. Unlike the company that bears that name today, it was a company whose shareholders' liability was limited by shares as opposed to guarantee. Its share capital of £3,000 was divided into 3,000 shares of £1 each and Colonel Du Pre was the majority shareholder. By July 1915 he was the holder of all the shares apart from those issued to the other directors as qualifying shares.

Three of the seven subscribers to the company became its first directors, namely, Colonel Du Pre himself, then a J.P. and modestly described in the Memorandum as of "No occupation", Montrose Cloete of "52, Berkley Square, W." also described as of "No occupation" and Charles Hinton Du Pre, "solicitor of 26, Essex Street, Strand".

> **Charles Du Pre** was a brother of Colonel Du Pre but, apart from being made an Honorary Member of the club in 1920, he does not feature again in any of the records of the club and he seems to have been involved only for the formalities of the club's incorporation as a company. There is a record of his having been a member of Burnham Beeches in 1911.

> **Montrose Cloete** was born in the Cape in 1860 into a family whose ancestors had left Holland for South Africa in 1658 for political reasons. In 1874, he came to England and was educated at Clifton College, and after that he travelled abroad extensively. Returning to England eventually he became an art critic and a respected judge of art and bric-à-brac. Although described in the company's Memorandum as of "No occupation", he was a partner in a firm of merchant bankers and became well known in the city. It was said of him that "the casual observer would never suspect the amount of financial knowledge and acumen concealed beneath his genial countenance". The Christian name "Montrose" reflects the connection through his paternal grandmother to the Montrose Grahams of the Fintry branch of the Clan Graham. Montrose Cloete was a cousin of the first Mrs. Du Pre and was Colonel Du Pre's stockbroker. He remained a director and a very active member of the Club until he died in 1933 at the age of seventy-three. It was he who, in 1929, presented the Club with the cup which bears his name and which, apart from the war years, has been played for every year since then.

Among the usual and widely worded "Objects" that are to be found in the Memorandum of Association of almost all companies, there were several that were specific to the purpose of this particular company. For example:

(A) To promote the game of golf and other athletic sports and pastimes.

(B) To acquire a lease of certain lands at Beaconsfield in the County of Buckingham for the purpose of building and laying out or completing a clubhouse and golf links thereon, and to establish and there carry on a club to be known as the Beaconsfield Golf Club ...

(C) To carry on the business of a Golf Club Company and in particular to lay out and prepare any lands for golf links or lawn tennis courts ...

(D) To buy, prepare, make, supply, sell and deal in all kinds of golf clubs or balls and all apparatus used in connection with golf and other athletic sports and all kinds of provisions and refreshments required or used by members of the club ...

The reference in (B) to "completing the clubhouse and golf links" is of particular interest because, given that the official opening of the new Club took place in July 1914, it is clear that work must have started on both the new clubhouse and the new course well before the legal formalities for the incorporation had been completed on 24th December 1913.

Although a new company was formed to take a lease of the course and clubhouse from Colonel Du Pre as the tenant for life of the Wilton Park estate, the Colonel's own special position in the new regime – he owned all but the directors' qualifying shares – was, understandably, recognised and preserved. For example, various specific provisions in the company's Articles of Association ensured that, for so long as he was a director of the company, he was to be the chairman of the Board of Directors and that, unlike other directors, he was not subject to retirement by rotation.

The Opening Exhibition Match

Despite the fact that the country, indeed the world, was on the very brink of war – in fact, the formal declaration came only three weeks later – the new golf club and course at Beaconsfield were opened in grand style on Saturday 18th July 1914 with an exhibition match involving two local professionals and two of the leading professionals of the day.

From the local scene were James Jones, the newly appointed professional at Beaconsfield, and H. R. Chestney, who was the professional at Burnham Beeches from 1901 to 1933. A minute of a meeting at his club held only a week before the match records that "Chestney was granted permission to play in a competition at the formal opening of Beaconsfield Golf Club on the 18th inst."

From the ranks of the top professionals came Ted Ray and none other than Harry Vardon himself.

Harry Vardon, Francis Ouimet and Ted Ray at the US Open Championship in 1913

By 1914, Ted Ray had played for England in nine professional matches against Scotland and, only two years earlier, had won the Open at Muirfield. In his book, *Only on Sundays*, Henry Longhurst recalls Ted Ray "with his felt hat turned up at the front and his pipe aglow, bashing at the ball as hard as mortal man could hit it and gouging the turf from the tee where his heels had twisted".

Harry Vardon had already won the Open five times and he was to win it again for the sixth and last time at Prestwick only a few days after the exhibition match at Beaconsfield. Having toured America together in 1913, Ray and Vardon were no strangers to each other in match play events, but it was while they were on that tour that they tied for first place in a stroke play tournament. That was the U.S. Open championship held that year at Brookline, Mass. They both tied with a twenty year old American amateur but, in the now celebrated play-off the next day, neither of them proved to be a match for the young amateur – by name, Francis Ouimet.

The morning round of the Beaconsfield exhibition match was a head-to-head single between the two Open champions which Ted Ray won at the 17th – having scored 71 to that point as against Vardon's 74. In the afternoon, Ted Ray and Chestney took on Vardon and Jones and, according to a contemporary account in the *South Bucks Free Press*, Ray and Chestney won "the fourball match with a score of 69 to Vardon and Jones' 72".

21

The local press account continued:

A very large and influential gathering witnessed the matches. Among those present were Lord Desborough (President of the Club), Colonel Du Pre, M.P., Mr. Montrose Cloete, the Reverend A. S. Commeline, Miss Du Pre, the Hon. H. I. Lawson, M.P., Mr. H. J. Johnston and Captain Fleetwood H. Pellew (Secretary). Lunch was served in the very imposing dining room at the new clubhouse and also in a marquee in the grounds and later tea was provided – the catering being in excellent style.

There is no mention of either the clubhouse architect, Stanley Hamp, or the course architect, Harry Colt, being present although they may well have been.

The New Home and its Architect

Being but a "shed", the clubhouse at the nine hole Wilton Park course probably made no claim to have been designed by anyone in particular or, indeed, by anyone at all. How different with the new clubhouse. Not only was it designed by an architect, it was designed by a very significant architect of the time, namely Stanley Hamp, a senior partner in the firm of Collcutt & Hamp, one of the leading London firms of architects. The firm now has its offices in Chesham. The enormous range and variety of the firm's work included the design of Wigmore Hall, the Savoy Hotel, the Adelphi, Sunningdale Ladies clubhouse and, most interestingly from the club's point of view, various buildings in Madras. It would be nice to think that the choice of Colcutt & Hamp to design the Beaconsfield clubhouse was in some way linked to the firm's work in Madras where one of Colonel Du Pre's ancestors was at one time Governor, but there is no evidence to support this. Hamp himself was Vice-President of the RIBA from 1935 to 1937 and died in 1968 at the age of ninety-one.

How far Hamp's design of the Beaconsfield clubhouse was determined or influenced by Colonel Du Pre is impossible to say, but happily it was a style reflecting the Arts and Craft Movement rather than any of his various other styles that was chosen – a style described succinctly by an architect who is a member of the Club as "Tudorbethan". Internally as well as externally there are reflections of the Arts and Craft Movement; the unexpected tiled surrounds to the fireplaces in the Members' Room and the Ladies' Dressing Room being particularly characteristic examples.

The excellence of Hamp's overall design and his sureness in the handling of its detail are plain to see. Some of the magnificent detailed working drawings for the clubhouse are on display in the Members' Room and in the Du Pre Room and amply reward a few moments study. At some stage, Stanley Hamp himself became a member of the Club and there is a copy letter on file dated 18th June 1919 in which the secretary informs Hamp that he would be re-admitted to membership on his return to England and payment of his subscription of seven guineas. Hamp did rejoin and for the next year or so continued to advise on suggested alterations to the clubhouse.

The distance between Seer Green Station and the clubhouse, though deliberately short, has been a matter on which, it seems, expert opinion has been sharply divided in the past. Writing in his appreciation of the course in 1925, Bernard Darwin[†] thought that the station was "within a putt of the clubhouse"; on the other hand, the editor of the golf magazine, *Tee Topics*, writing in August 1932, felt that the two were "within half a mashie shot" of each other.

What Stanley Hamp must have thought privately at being commissioned to design such an imposing structure immediately next to a railway track is not recorded, but the plan for the clubhouse that he produced was certainly well worked out. It permitted an easy progression for the golfer, whether a man or a woman, from the railway station or the car park to the caddie-master's house,[††] then to the clubhouse and the changing rooms and on to the 1st tee where, hopefully, the caddie would be waiting with the clubs and other impedimenta of the game. The reverse was true on completion of the round for, after leaving the 18th green, the caddie could take the clubs to the caddie shed for cleaning while the golfer could continue his or her way back to the changing rooms and refreshment. And the plan works just as well today as it did then – even though caddie-carts have long since replaced the luxury of caddies.

The exterior of the clubhouse is built of handmade clay facing bricks and has a clay tiled roof with distinctive "hipped" ends. Purpose-made bricks were used for the door and window surrounds, for the mullions, for the circular columns on the terrace outside the lounge and for the chimney stacks. The principal bond of the brickwork consists of header courses interspersed with five courses of stretchers – a bond technically known as "English Garden Wall".

It is clear from the working drawings that the dining room balcony with its decorative balustrade consisting of vertical and diagonal timber frames with infilled brick panels was intended to be a central and prominent feature of the original design. And when, on sunny days, the canopy over the balcony was unfurled the clubhouse must, indeed, have been a most impressive sight. Sadly, for reasons of safety, the balustrade was removed in the early 1970s and access to the balcony has been not been permitted since then. All that is now left to remind members of earlier times on the

[†]*The Beaconsfield Golf Club* by Bernard Darwin published by The Golf Clubs' Association in 1925.
[††]The original carved timber plaques "Caddie Master" are retained on the wall of the building.

The Clubhouse, July 1947, showing the balcony and the pierced brick parapet

balcony are the wall bell (now disconnected) for summoning the steward and the newer bricks inserted into the wall where the canopy fittings used to be.

Above the balcony and the twin bow windows is a parapet behind which the roof joins the walls of the building. A photograph of the clubhouse that appeared in *Golf Illustrated* in July 1947 shows that the parapet was still in the same pierced brick style in which it had been built. By contrast, a photograph taken on the occasion of Angela Ward's winning of the British Girls Championship at Beaconsfield in September 1955 shows that the parapet was no longer in the pierced brick style and had been rebuilt with solid brickwork in accordance with the original drawings. This was probably done for reasons both of safety and ease of maintenance.

The obvious symmetry of the exterior of the clubhouse, though now somewhat lost in more recent modifications, is substantially repeated in the interior with the centrepiece lounge on the ground floor being flanked on the one side by the ladies' changing facilities and, on the other side, by those for the men. It may be thought, perhaps, to be a somewhat surprising feature of the house that the splendid east wing that parallels the last part of the 18th hole and overlooks the 18th green should have been designed to accommodate staff quarters. In fact, as is explained later, much of this east wing did not form part of the original design and was a later addition to the main building.

Undoubtedly the most outstanding feature of the whole house is the first floor dining room with its extensive views over the course through the French doors and its beautifully proportioned hammer beam roof with gargoyle-like demon faces ("grotesques") to each of the hammer beams. It is a room to which Hamp must have given great thought, and it is a room that, ever since, has given countless hundreds of members and visitors many hours of frustration trying to fathom the mysteries of the animals depicted at regular intervals on the plaster frieze around the room, and to decode the initials that appear in the frieze over the fireplaces. What, they wonder, is the significance of the owl and the rabbit? What is that other bird? What is the significance of the Chinese or Indian-like face that is also featured at regular intervals – does he reflect the family's connections with Madras? While the initials "SH" are probably those of Stanley Hamp, who were "GB", "BR", "PP" and all the others? Craftsmen perhaps? Relatives of the Du Pres perhaps? Or who? All efforts to find answers to these questions have so far been singularly unsuccessful.

A section of the plaster frieze in the dining room

One of the fearsom "grotesques" in the dining room

And So to War!

Sadly, there are no Club records or other sources of information as to what happened after the official opening event on 18th July 1914 and during the ensuing years of the First World War – indeed, it is not possible to pick up the story of the Club again until 5th July 1919 for that is the day on which the first Board meeting was held for which minutes still exist.

Colonel Du Pre himself had seen active military service in the Boer War and was involved again in the First World War when he served with the Royal Horse Artillery (TF Reserve) in the Middle East and elsewhere. Captain Pellew, the Club's first secretary, was called up for military service, as was Jones, the Club's professional. Moreover, many of the Club's members as well as its other staff were also involved in the war effort and, after the exhilarating opening event only a few weeks earlier, it must have been deeply

The Beaconsfield Vineyard, Quebec

saddening to see the brand new clubhouse and course almost deserted for the next four years.

In his book about the history of Burnham Beeches Golf Club, Michael Roe alludes to the fact that the First World War started less than three weeks after the official opening of Beaconsfield Golf Club, and writes, "Happily our neighbouring club thrived despite the inauspicious timing of its birth." Inauspicious it was, but the neighbouring club did eventually thrive – even though a fresh start had to be made when peace had been restored.

Beaconsfield Golf Club Inc.

Before concluding this chapter on the opening of Beaconsfield Golf Club in the United Kingdom, it is appropriate to recognise that this is not the only, or indeed the first, golf club to bear that name, for "Beaconsfield Golf Club Inc." was incorporated in the Province of Quebec on 25th May 1904. In 1874, a certain John Henry Menzies acquired property in the district of Pointe Claire, Quebec, and in honour of his good friend, Benjamin Disraeli, Earl of Beaconsfield, Menzies named his new homestead Beaconsfield. Although his attempt to establish a commercial vineyard there from grapes imported from America, France and Italy did not succeed because of the harsh Quebec winters, the village, now city, that then developed in that neighbourhood became known as Beaconsfield and it was in that area that the Tooke family came to have a summer residence. The interest in golf of Arthur Tooke and others of the family led to the golf course at Beaconsfield being developed and it was his father, Benjamin, who became its first president.

Reciprocal arrangements between the two clubs have existed for many years – indeed, as early as 1937 the secretary received a letter from the "Beaconsfield Club in Montreal" thanking the Club for the courtesy of the course that had been extended to its members and hoping that the exchange of correspondence would continue. Since then, several members of each club have visited the other and have been most warmly received. The Canadian Club celebrates its own centenary in 2004.

Chapter Four

Harry Colt and His Course

*Among the new courses in the Home Counties there is none that
can excel, nor even equal in the opinion of many good judges, the
picturesque course of the Beaconsfield Golf Club at Seer Green.*

[*The Car, 13th January 1921*]

Harry Shapland Colt 1869–1951

IF COLONEL DU PRE's selection of Stanley Hamp as the architect to design the
new clubhouse demonstrated his commitment to making Beaconsfield a
golf club of high standing, then his selection of Harry Colt as the course
architect underscored that commitment many times.

Colt learned to play golf as a boy at The Worcestershire Golf Club and was
a proficient golfer by the time he went up to Clare College, Cambridge, in
1887 to read law. While there, he participated fully in the activities of the
University Golf Club and, in due course, became its captain. Having
graduated, served his Articles and become a solicitor, Colt joined a firm of
solicitors in Hastings and became a partner in 1894. By then, he had already
become a member of the R&A and had won the Gold Vase in 1891 playing
off a handicap of 2 and again in 1893 playing off scratch. While in Hastings,
Colt continued with his various golfing activities and became increasingly
interested in golf course design – his appetite having no doubt been whetted
by his involvement in the design of Rye golf course in 1894. Colt was still with
the Hastings firm when, in 1901, the newly opened Sunningdale Golf Club
advertised for the position of secretary – for which Colt, together with 434
other people, applied. Following the whittling down process, which
concluded with dinner at the Café Monico in Piccadilly Circus for the last six
candidates, Colt was eventually selected for the position at a salary of £150
per annum.

Over the next few years Colt became more and more occupied with golf
course design and modification. At first, he kept an appropriate balance
between his responsibilities as secretary at Sunningdale and his extra-mural
activities, which were always carried out with the knowledge and agreement
of the Sunningdale committee. But his success and reputation as a course

Harry Shapland Colt, 1869-1951

architect spread rapidly and by 1909 he was in such considerable demand that, in effect, his position at Sunningdale had become part-time and the final break with Sunningdale came in 1913. Even so, the parting was on an entirely cordial basis as is borne out by the fact that Colt remained a consultant adviser to the Club's Green Committee for some years afterwards.

It is said that, in those days, Colt's activities in connection with each new course he designed would usually extend over a two year period before the opening date. On that basis, it is likely that he accepted the commission from Colonel Du Pre to design a new course at Beaconsfield even before his final separation from the Sunningdale Club had taken place. By the time he left Sunningdale, Colt had already designed some twenty courses including those at Alwoodley, Le Touquet, Stoke Poges, Denham,† Northants County,† Swinley Forest, The Eden at St Andrews, Pine Valley, N.J., St Georges Hill,† Burhill, Camberley Heath,† and Puerta de Hierro, Madrid.

Colt was the first course architect of any significance not to have been a professional golfer but he was, of course, as good a golfer as many of the professionals. In conjunction with various partners such as Dr. Alister Mackenzie, Charles Alison and John Morrison, Colt went on to design over 300 courses in some sixteen countries and beyond doubt he became one of the leading course architects of the time. Years later after Colt had died, Henry Longhurst wrote in his book, *Only On Sundays*, "I have always suspected that the late Harry Colt was the best golf architect of all time." Many would agree.

The New Course

Unfortunately, none of Colt's plans or drawings for the new course at Beaconsfield has survived nor is there even a description as to the sort of land that Colt had to work with. Although much of the land on the Du Pre estate

---

†It is likely that Charles H. Alison, who was secretary at Stoke Poges in those days, but who later became a celebrated course architect in his own right, was Colt's pupil assistant in the design of these particular courses.

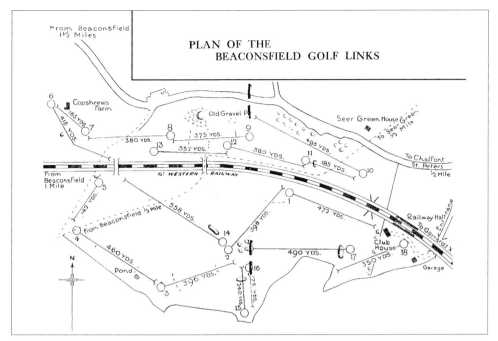

A plan of the course before the 3rd, 8th and 15th tees were repositioned

was farmland and although there is evidence, for example on the 3rd and 4th holes, that at some time in the past ridge farming had taken place in that area, it is likely that most of the area covered by the course was parkland rather than farmed land.

The only known description of the new course as it was when it was opened in 1914, is to be found in the *South Bucks Free Press* report of the Vardon and Ray exhibition match played on 18th July 1914:

> The first four holes are noteworthy for their ingenuousness of their bunkers and other difficulties and the next nine are better still for the spirit of adventure that they engender. At the sixth, the sensation of driving over a deep hollow, if driven well, is splendidly consumated by the playing of a brassie shot over a precipitous and wondrous drop of forty feet in the fairway. The seventh is an excellent hole, while a deep valley and a large natural pit come into consideration at the eighth, and two imposing rows of bunkers greet the eye from the ninth tee. The tenth is played along the slope of a hill, the left hand side of which has been raised twenty-nine feet for a distance of 200 yards, so as to prevent the ball from running down: and the eleventh boasts an immense natural bunker, forty feet deep. The other holes are equally interesting. The park is extremely picturesque and is beautifully wooded while the air is bracing and salubrious.

Although over the years several changes of detail have been made to the course, no major modification in its general layout, or indeed to any individual hole, has taken place.

Allowing for the usual errors of measurement in the early days and for the fact that the tees at some holes have obviously been relocated, a comparison of the yardage of the holes in the original layout with those of the course today (figures in brackets) as measured from the white tees shows a remarkable similarity.

	Yards		Bogey		Yards		Bogey
1st	440	(451)	5	10th	470	(480)	5
2nd	375	(366)	4	11th	175	(176)	3
3rd	375	(378)	4	12th	380	(357)	5
4th	460	(508)	5	13th	345	(350)	4
5th	175	(163)	3	14th	520	(539)	5
6th	400	(430)	5	15th	210	(283)	4
7th	185	(175)	3	16th	179	(202)	3
8th	380	(378)	5	17th	420	(510)	5
9th	360	(355)	4	18th	350	(392)	4
Out	3170	(3204)	38	In	3049	(3289)	38
				Out	3170	(3204)	38
				Total	6219	(6493)	76

One of the desirable, almost obligatory, characteristics of course design until well into the second half of the last century was that the tees should be constructed close to the green of the preceding hole. Moreover, it was customary to have several relatively small tees rather than one large tee – the purpose being to provide variety and flexibility. In this respect Beaconsfield was a model of contemporary design and even though over the years different philosophies and improvements in equipment have led to changes in the size and location of many of the tees, evidence of these early design features can still be seen at Beaconsfield, particularly at the 4th, 8th, 13th and 16th.

Deception and Uncertainty

Every course architect has his own philosophy about general course design and specific design features. Some of these remain more or less unchanged throughout his career while others change in response to fashion and his own experiences.

In his earlier years, Colt was given to designing greens that were broadly round and flat and most of the greens on his early courses, including those at Beaconsfield, reflect that approach. Colt was not much given to blind holes, but he regarded features intended to deceive the player or to create uncertainty in his mind as fair game. A good example of this is to be found at the 1st hole where the green is set deceptively further back from the top of the rising ground than would appear and the forward location of the bunkers adds to this deception. How often are approaches to this green left short? Again, the ridge in front of the 2nd green was placed there to create uncertainty in the player's mind as to how far the green is beyond the ridge. The same effect is achieved on the 3rd hole where the slightly raised plateau area stretching some forty yards in front of the green has a foreshortening effect.

Diagonal Cross-bunkers

Many changes have been made over the years to the number, size and position of bunkers on the course and it is now impossible to know or to work out where all the bunkers on the original course were located. Suffice it to say that, in order to reduce maintenance costs and to accommodate the distances achievable with improving equipment, several bunkers have been relocated or removed. At one time, there were well over 100 bunkers on the course, but today only seventy-eight are left.

Fortunately, the course still retains several excellent examples of what was probably Colt's most distinctive design feature in his earlier years – diagonal rows of cross-bunkers.

The design philosophy of this feature is that a diagonal row of bunkers presents the player with a choice; on the one hand he can take the shorter, relatively safe route over the near bunkers in which case he has a more difficult or longer next shot or, on the other hand, he can take on the longer carry in the hope of reaping reward on the other side. Diagonal cross-bunkers, as opposed to horizontal cross-bunkers, also enable a course to be played with more equal challenge by both long and short hitters of the ball.

The first of these Colt "trademarks" at Beaconsfield faces the player on the tee at the 2nd hole. When the course was first opened, the tees for this hole were to the left of the 1st green rather than to the back of it as they are today, and it is still just possible to discern one of the original tees among the subsequently planted fir trees to the left. With the tees in that position, this row of diagonal cross-bunkers appearing so early in the round presented a considerable challenge. Despite the subsequent relocation of the tees, the effect of the diagonal placing of these bunkers can still be appreciated – if that is the right word!

Similarly at the 9th tee, a diagonal row of bunkers faces the player, although with the recent closure of the bunker on the extreme right hand side, the challenge has been somewhat reduced. Originally, and certainly until 1925, the 9th tee presented the player with a much greater challenge than it does today for, as can be seen in a photograph that was featured in Bernard Darwin's 1925 appreciation of the course, a double row of cross-bunkers awaited the player – and altogether there were thirteen bunkers on

The double row of cross bunkers at the 9th as illustrated in Darwin's 1925 appreciation of the course

that hole. At some unknown later date, the first row was removed, though not without leaving still discernible traces of where they used to be.

At the 13th, 14th and 17th diagonal bunkers originally faced the player on the tee but at the 13th and 17th most of the bunkers forming those rows have since been removed. For example, in 1935, it was decided that "the centre cross-bunkers on the 14th and the 17th holes should be removed allowing a reasonable fairway in the middle with bunkers on either side". Other bunkers in those rows were removed later on. Diagonal rows of cross-bunkers that menace fairway shots still exist at the 13th and 14th holes.

"The actual course is on the whole clear of trees"

Beaconsfield is a park golf course and one of the prettiest to be found anywhere. When a golf course is praised overmuch for the beauty of its scenery and the goodness of its lunch, an uneasy suspicion arises that the golf is not very good. It behoves one to be very careful. Nevertheless, I will take the risk and declare that the beech woods at Beaconsfield are extraordinarily beautiful and it is quite impossible to think of the course without thinking of them also. Moreover, they are not only beautiful but kind, they may catch a criminal hook or slice now and again, but they do not get unduly in the way. The actual course is on the whole clear of trees.

So began Bernard Darwin's 1925 commendation of the Beaconsfield course. In a similar vein, the editor of the golf magazine *Tee Topics* wrote in his issue for August 1932, after a visit to Beaconsfield: "There are trees too but they are

Looking across the 2nd green to the 3rd green in the far distance. Notice the absence of trees on both sides of the 3rd (photo late 1930s)

guides rather than menaces; in other words, they are not too pestilentially numerous nor do they impinge so close upon the line of play that the golfer goes about his shot in sheer dread."

The number and variety of trees that form the wide, yet private, corridors of most of the holes have been a feature of the Beaconsfield course for a long time but, as photographs taken in the earlier years show, this was not always the case. When it was first opened, the course was nothing like as wooded as it has since become and the holes were not tree lined as they are today. Even in the early 1950s, it was possible to stand on the 4th tee and see players crossing the bridge to the 6th tee. In fact, only a relatively small proportion of the trees on the course today are fifty years old and even fewer are seventy or a hundred years old and most of the older trees are on the boundaries of the course.

While many of the trees that exist today were self–sown, ever since the mid-1950s the Club has pursued a continuous policy of tree planting and welfare in close collaboration with English Woodland and the English Forestry Commission and with the help of Forestry Commission grants. The first of several tree planting programmes undertaken in conjunction with the Forestry Commission took place in 1955 and covered part of the area between the 4th and 14th holes at a cost of some £200. Several other such programmes were undertaken over the next two decades. The one in 1964,

View from the hill at the 8th looking across the 8th tees and the 7th green to the 6th green in the far distance (photo "Tee Topics" 1932)

for example, included the planting of mixtures of birch, ash, cherry and Lawson Cypress between the 17th fairway and the practice ground (40 trees), between the 9th and 12th fairways (20 trees), and to the left of the 16th green to form a copse of twenty-five trees.

In addition to these larger scale programmes, smaller tree projects have been undertaken at various times. These have included:

– the planting of evergreen trees to shield the 1st tee from the visitors' car park.

– the planting in 1967 at the suggestion of the then captain of a willow tree beside the pond at the 4th hole.

– the replacement of the bunker at driving distance on the right hand side of the 6th fairway by the copse at the top of the hill.

– the formation, at the suggestion of the head greenkeeper, Bob Plain, of a spinney at the back of the 17th green.

– the creation in 1978 of an evergreen screening hedge at the back of the 1st green and, "depending on the golfing area between the two", another such screen between the 3rd green and the 4th tee. [Fortunately, there was not enough room for the latter hedge to be planted and recently the Leylandii trees at the back of the 1st green have been removed and replaced with more appropriate trees and shrubs.]

– the creation of copses between the 15th and 16th holes.

The Club's tree policy over the last forty years or so has produced a much more attractive and scenic course than it was originally and it is unquestionably the most significant change and the greatest improvement to the course that has taken place since it opened in 1914.

A Much Discussed Bunker

Of the few design modifications that have taken place over the years, perhaps the most interesting one occurred at the 3rd hole. In his discussion of the course published in 1925, Bernard Darwin wrote:

> At the third, there is a tree to the left of the fairway which exercises rather a magnetic influence; even the chronic slicer feels suddenly impelled to hook. If, however, we can resist the tree, we should have a four, for there is a fine big green and plenty of room to pitch and stop.

In his later, revised version published in 1947, the description of the 3rd hole was amended to read:

> At the third we should have a four, for there is a fine big green and plenty of room in which to pitch and stop; but there is a much discussed bunker in the middle of the fairway which must be carried or circumvented, and there are handicap golfers who, looking from their drive up the slope to the distant green, dispute the official length of 385 yards.

The original tee for the 3rd hole was located at the back of the 2nd green more or less where the 15th medal tee now stands. At that time, the 3rd hole was perfectly straight with the existing first bunker on the right hand side of the fairway being visible from the tee just beyond the ridge that still exists. In November 1935, it was decided that the hole should be "played dog-leg from tees near the 14th green and utilising the present fairway". In other words, the decision was to move the tees some distance over to the right to where the yellow tee is today. This decision was implemented in the 1938-1939 winter programme and involved:

– building a new tee on the right of the present tee.
– extending the fairway to the right and close in the fairway on the left.
– extending the first bunker on the right and also the second bunker on the right.
– building a new bunker on the left of the fairway 180 yards from the tee.
– building a new bunker twenty yards short of the green on the right and in line with the present bunkers.

Thus, the realignment of the fairway from the left to the right meant that the bunker that had been on the right hand side of the fairway became the "much discussed bunker in the middle of the fairway" that Darwin found in 1947. The implied criticism in his remarks about this bunker must have added to the discussion, but it was not until 1958 that the Board asked the

Green Committee to review the layout of the 3rd hole. The resulting proposal was approved in 1960 and the 3rd hole became the hole that it is today although some of the bunkers have since been removed.

And the 15th Hole

Almost since the opening of the course in 1914, the 15th hole seems to have presented problems of one kind or another, but less so to the player than to the greenkeeper. The principal problem was and to some extent still is one of percolating water and poor drainage which manifests itself most obviously in the casual water that frequently collects during winter months in the low lying ground that crosses both the 15th and 16th holes. This is by no means a new phenomenon, for as early as the winter of 1923 the Ladies' Committee was asking for a plank and a net to be placed on the hole to enable balls to be retrieved from the casual water. Maybe the long skirts that lady golfers wore at that time added to their difficulties in this respect.

The presence on the course in 1968 of the Gas Board's trenching equipment enabled an "arrangement" to be made to have the 15th drained, and that might well have resolved the problem had it not been for the construction later that year of a new car park at Wilton Park on the raised ground behind the green. The Board was convinced that rainwater drained off this car park, percolated down the 15th, collected in the hollow at the bottom of the slope and overwhelmed the new drainage work. Therefore, in January 1969, the captain wrote to the commandant at Wilton Park about the matter. A meeting with the commandant led to the pond beside the 15th green (which at that time was on military property) being cleared and dredged in the belief that the percolating water would drain into it. The matter was taken no further than that – but the problem remained. Indeed, it still remains, although with the 15th medal tee repositioned as it is today, the area where the casual water collects is less of a problem.

The accumulation of casual water, however, was not the only problem with the 15th hole. Reciting the problems of the 15th green as being poor drainage, little or no rootzone, considerable meadow grass and too few pin positions, the 1991 five year plan for the greens called for the green to be completely lifted and relayed in 1993-1994. By the time this part of the programme came to be implemented, the Club had purchased the pond area to the right of the green and so the course architect was asked to redesign the entire hole. His design has been a distinct improvement on what previously existed but, despite the green having been constructed to current specifications and despite the fact that the turf from the original green was deliberately re-used to minimise any difference in speed, it is still not without its problems.

The 15th green in the late 1930s

The Short Holes

It is a generally accepted principal of golf course design that, wherever possible, the short holes on a course should face in different directions so as to provide variation according to wind direction and that they should be of different lengths – or at least play as if they were of different lengths. The four short holes at Beaconsfield (five if the 15th is included as a short hole) follow the first of these precepts fairly closely, but much less so the second if only the yardage is considered. From time to time over the years, members have criticised the short holes at Beaconsfield as being too similar in length – at least on a calm day – and looking only at the original length of the four short holes, there was some substance in the criticism because all four holes measured between 175 and 185 yards.

The matter seems to have been raised first at Committee level in 1923 and at the following meeting it was decided that the 11th and 16th holes should remain as they were, but that temporary forward tees at the 5th and 7th should be constructed and used for a six month trial period after which the matter would be considered again.

That seemingly sensible decision seems to have generated considerable feeling among some members of the Club because, even before the trial period was over, the number and nature of the complaints was such that the Committee decided that there should be "alternative tees at all four short holes so that the length of each hole could be varied from time to time". Although this matter reared its head again occasionally in subsequent years, the provision at each short hole of a variety of tees at significantly different distances seems to have resolved most members' concerns and to have provided sufficient flexibility.

And a Further 9 Holes?

The question of constructing an additional nine holes has been discussed on several occasions.

The first time was in 1934, when the Committee resolved "to recommend for consideration by the Directors the feasibility of making an additional nine holes in view of the congestion at week-ends". However, Colonel Du Pre seemingly had other ideas about spending money for at the next meeting he informed the Committee that:

> The Directors had decided that they could not sanction the proposed alterations and additions to the course at that time but that, in view of the two years drought, it would be better to concentrate on renovation work on the tees, approaches, fairways and bunkers – particular attention being paid to the tees.

Two years later, in 1936, the Committee received a letter from a member complaining that he and several members felt that, owing to the large number of matches, they were often debarred from playing a quiet round during the week and suggested that a nine hole course would be of some help. Alternatively, the letter said, five-day members could be allowed to play after 5 p.m. on Saturdays and Sundays when the course was usually empty. While pointing out that the latter suggestion was not possible, the Committee obviously had some sympathy with the basic point that was being made and eventually agreed to send the following resolution to the Board of Directors:

> Owing to the fact that there have been so many complaints from members, followed in some cases by resignations, owing to the congestion on the course, the Committee unanimously recommend to the Directors the advisability of laying out an additional nine holes.

The same issue was raised on several subsequent occasions, the most recent being in 1990 when the firm of John Jacobs & Associates was asked to inspect the course and neighbouring land and to report on the feasibility of adding an additional nine holes. Although the report was optimistic, the matter was not progressed further.

It has been the Club's policy for several years to seek to purchase adjoining land whenever feasible and appropriate both for the protection of the Club's boundaries and also to provide space on which to develop alternative or additional holes should that become necessary or desirable. The most recent purchase of the forty acres of land between the 18th hole and Potkiln Lane is a reflection of that continuing policy of insurance. It is also an interesting example of the Club buying further land that at one time formed part of the Wilton Park estate.

Finishing at the 10th by Val Doonican

The Du Pre Coat of Arms

The clubhouse in the 1980s

*One of the fearsome "grotesques"
in the dining room*

A section of plaster frieze in the dining room

40

An aerial photograph of the course, circa 1970s

The putting green and the 1st tee on a frosty morning

"Golf Cottage" (formerly known as "The Seventh")

Autumn colours on the course

An autumn view of the 10th from the 11th green

43

Chapter Five

The Keepers of the Green

ACCORDING TO the first edition of *The Golfer's Handbook* to be published after the First World War, T. H. Dosset was the greenkeeeper at Beaconsfield but it is doubtful if he was anything more than a groundsman.

In those days, it was not uncommon for the club professional to be responsible for directing and supervising the activities of those who worked on the course and who, as in the early Beaconsfield records, were usually referred to as "groundsmen" or "the outside men". It is known that, at least by 1920, Beaconsfield's first professional, James Jones, had been given this responsibility, for that year the Club secretary wrote to the local tax surveyor apologising for not having included in the return that he had made in respect of Jones the sum of £50 per annum that Jones was paid "for supervision of the course". The 1921 edition of *The Golfer's Handbook* names Jones as both the professional and the greenkeeper.

Motorised mowing machines had been developed before the end of the nineteenth century and from the outset of the new course Beaconsfield had at least two 30" Ransome mowers for cutting the greens. But for fairways and heavy cutting, much reliance was still placed on horse-drawn mowers with the horses wearing leather or rubber "shoes" to prevent surface damage.

Beaconsfield had at least two horses in those early days and on 2nd October 1919 there was an accident involving one of them, a gelding named "Podgy". At 8.30 a.m. that morning, Podgy was pulling a mowing machine from the 12th down to the 10th fairway when the machine began to slide. In trying to stop the machine turning over, Sidney Lidgley, the groundsman who was leading Podgy at the time, tried to stop it but ended up twisting his ankle and breaking several bones. With a medical note from Dr. Turner of Wycombe End, Sidney was off work for several weeks during which time, with the approval of its insurers, the Club continued to pay his wage of £2 per week. Alas, a worse fate awaited Podgy for shortly after the incident he developed a lameness which, in the vet's view, meant that he was unfit to work and should be destroyed. Accordingly, Podgy was put down, but when the Club claimed under its Livestock Insurance Policy, there were a few anxious weeks before the claim was accepted because the insurers "proved difficult" about not being informed before the horse had been put down. This incident brought to light the fact that the Club's other horse, "Nobby", was not covered by any insurance at all and this omission was hastily corrected – albeit with a different insurer.

In 1923, the name of J. Weston appears in *The Golfer's Handbook* as the greenkeeper at Beaconsfield. "Old Weston", as he appears to have been affectionately known by everyone including Colonel Du Pre, retired in December 1945 after what

Bob Plain, head greenkeeper from 1957 to 1980

the Colonel recalled had been more than thirty years as a greenkeeper, and the Board granted him a retirement pension of 10s. a week. Old Weston may have been the head greenkeeper for several years, but by 1933, when Percy Alliss had become the professional, the position of head greenkeeper was held by "A. E. Berry" even though Old Weston was still on the staff. The distribution list for the Club's Christmas Fund for that year shows that Berry, as greenkeeper, received £12.10s. whereas J. Weston, as one of the nine "groundsmen", received only £7.2s.6d.

Ted Berry was one of three brothers who were members of the Artisans section for many years from the late 1920s, and all three were very competent golfers (see Chapter Fifteen). As head greenkeeper, Ted enjoyed rent free occupation of Seer Green View – one of the two semi-detached properties on Farm Lane that were included in the club's lease. Ted remained at the Club during the Second World War and, when various members of the Club staff were called up for war service, he took on various other responsibilities including that of caddie-master. Someone who was a boy caddie during the war still remembers the somewhat austere manner with which Ted controlled "the lads".

It was probably because of Ted Berry's failing health that a new greenkeeper, Bob Plain, was appointed to the staff at the end of 1956 and it was only two months later that Ted became too ill to continue work. When, sadly, Ted died early in April 1957, Bob Plain, who had previously been at Hartsbourne and Harefield Place, was promoted to head greenkeeper and became the first member of the staff to occupy the new bungalow, Greenfield, that the Club was then having built in Seer Green.

It was during Bob's era that the Club's extensive tree planting schemes were primarily implemented, and it was also during his time with the Club that the disturbances of laying the North Sea gas pipe-line across the 18th and 1st holes, under the railway, and then on across the 11th and 10th holes, occurred.

In November 1977, the greenkeepers' premises, which have always been located where they are today, were totally destroyed by a fire thought to have been deliberately started by the same firebug who set fire to the Seer Green school a few days later. Although a Green Goddess from Wilton Park was quickly on the scene, it was too late to save the equipment, including the 1946 Ferguson tractor which is believed to have been the only one of its kind left in the country. New sheds were constructed in the same location and were ready for use the following October.

There is an artificial-looking mound on the left of the 12th fairway some thirty yards or so short of the 150 yard marker post. At one time there had been a tree on that site and when it was felled its stump and roots had been left in the ground. These roots frequently caused damage to the gang mowers and so, in 1978, Bob was authorised in 1978 to grub them out provided that he "leave a mound as this could be a feature and possibly something to aim at".

By 1964, the Standard Scratch Score for the course was established by the EGU as 71, but a later measurement of the course "on the horizontal plane" showed that it was eighty-two yards short of the minimum distance for a SSS of 71. The choice was to accept a new SSS of 70 or to lengthen the course. Being anxious to retain the current rating, the Green Committee instructed Bob Plain to prepare proposals for lengthening the course. Bob's proposals were accepted with the result that the course was lengthened by eighty-three yards. A new 4th tee was constructed further back to add thirty-two yards and make it a par 5 under the new criteria. [The Board initially had concerns about the tee's proximity to the 3rd green.]. A new tee at the 17th was constructed on the other side of the copse behind the 16th green to add thirty-nine yards and make it a par 5. The new temporary tee at the 16th was made the permanent medal tee thus adding at least twelve yards.

Thus the SSS remained at 71 as it is today.

Those who have served on Green Committees will not need to be told how arduous a task it is and how demanding meetings can be. The meeting held on the evening of Friday 23rd November 1979, at the home of its Chairman, Don McIntosh, and attended by its other members, Roger Ames, John Woods

The greenkeeping staff – Summer 2002
Left to right: Tony Hore, Michael Homer, Bill Paterson (head greenkeeper), James Lillitou and
David Reid (deputy head greenkeeper)
Chris Lillitou (inset) was on vacation when the photograph was taken

and Bob Plain, bears testimony to this fact. The minutes for what had clearly been a most difficult meeting end with the words: "There being no further business, the meeting ended well into the Saturday morning – a bottle and a half of malt whiskey after it started."

In no way connected with that meeting, Bob Plain tendered his resignation in 1980 and joined Hazlemere to supervise the construction of that course and to become its head greenkeeper.

Michael Merrick, who had been Bob's deputy for some time, succeeded him as head greenkeeper and remained in the post for five years.

Bill Paterson was selected to be the next head greenkeeper by a sub-committee comprising Bill Houston, Ken Kingshott and Michael Hunter, the secretary, and he took up his duties in November 1985.

Bill had served his apprenticeship and held positions as assistant greenkeeper at various Scottish clubs before taking up the post of head greenkeeper/course manager at the Randpark Club in South Africa in 1971. Returning to this country, he was head greenkeeper at the Vale of Leven and then at Royal Dornoch, where he prepared the course for the British Amateur Championship in 1985 before leaving for his new post at Beaconsfield.

Bill Paterson supervises construction of the new bunker on the right of the 2nd fairway

In addition to the considerable changes in greenkeeping equipment and technology that have occurred in recent years, Bill and his staff have been involved in three major projects on the course.

The Driving Range

The first practice ground was part of the original design, but as early as 1936 the secretary was instructed to "arrange an additional practice ground between the 1st and 17th fairways to be earmarked for Kenyon [the professional] and his assistants for giving lessons". In 1946, the Green Committee agreed to keep the suggestion of creating "a penthouse on the practice ground to provide shelter in wet weather when the second practice ground was clear" under consideration and this idea was in fact discussed on several subsequent occasions although nothing materialised. It was not until 1990 that the Board accepted the Green Committee's strong recommendation to develop a driving range on the second practice ground and, after a successful trial period (and not a few negative voices) the driving range was constructed and brought into operation in 1994. It has proved to be a facility of considerable benefit, not only to the professionals giving lessons, but also to members of all levels of ability, and it will be even more useful now that the "penthouse" has become a reality.

The Bunker Renovation Programme

The much appreciated VAT refund on members' subscriptions in 1995 was used by the Club, as by most clubs, for the benefit of members. At Beaconsfield, this took the form of improving the quality of the course by undertaking an extensive bunker renovation programme. It was a three year phased programme in which virtually all of the bunkers were either reconstructed in the original Colt style, relocated or closed as being no longer "in play", and in which the process of shaping the fairways was started. The whole programme, developed by the course architects, Hawtree, in conjunction with the Green Committee and Bill Paterson, made considerable additional demands on all the greenkeeping staff and to them and to those artisan members who also took part must go due appreciation.

Fairway Irrigation

At the time of Bill's appointment, the Club had taken the decision in principle to extend the greens irrigation system to cover the tees, and it fell to Bill to supervise its installation and the up-dating and rewiring of the existing system by the contractors. Even so, that irrigation system had its limitations since the water was drawn from the mains supply which was expensive, and unreliable in drought conditions. Moreover, legislation in the early 1990s enabled Water Authorities to restrict the supply of mains water to playing fields, golf courses, and the like. Such restrictions were in fact imposed in the long dry summer of 1995 and caused serious problems on the course. Fortunately, after several unsuccessful applications, the Club was granted permission to test bore for water on its land and the successful outcome led to a water extraction licence being granted, not only to supply the existing irrigation system, but also an extended system to cover fairways and approach areas. The installation and up-grading of the whole system in 1998 was again supervised by Bill and his team.

The presentation of the course and, following the expert ecological appraisal of the course carried out during the winter of 1998-1999, the protection of the environment are two aspects of greenkeeping that have come very much to the fore in recent years, and will continue to demand the attention of the head greenkeeper at Beaconsfield as elsewhere.

"to the 6th ... from the 5th by Val Doonican

Chapter Six

Years of Growth
1919 to 1939 – Management, Membership and Matters of the House

ALTHOUGH THE First World War ended in November 1918, it was well into the following year before Colonel Du Pre and those members and staff who had been on war service returned and a new start could be made. But the task of building up a Club worthy of the new clubhouse and course was not going to be an easy one, for the war years had taken their toll not least on the financial situation of the Club. That the financial situation was difficult is well reflected in the secretary's letter acknowledging the receipt of a new local rating assessment as from 1st July 1919. He wrote to the rating assessor saying:

> I think it would be very hard on the Club if the assessment was raised. During the war, the Club has been carried on at a loss to the Company and the owner of the ground has had to forego all rent for the last five years. The new financial year is just starting and I think with the increase of cost of labour and materials, it is quite doubtful if the Company will be able to pay the reduced rent of £300. In these circumstances I consider that to raise the assessment would have a prejudicial effect on the Club.

There is no record of the rating assessor's response, but in a follow-up letter later the same month the secretary advised him of two changes† to the clubhouse but expressed the view that they should not involve an increase in the rating assessment. In August, the secretary sent the assessor a cheque for £49.16s.8d. in payment of the rates and informed him that the landlord (Colonel Du Pre) had agreed to a permanent reduction in the rent from £675 to £300 per annum "as he does not see any chance of receiving the full amount previously agreed upon without crippling the Club".

From this correspondence the magnitude of the task facing the management of the Club in the years immediately after the war is obvious,

---

†The two changes were the construction of a cellar and the covering over of the "caddie-boys yard" with a flat roof. The cellar, together with the two empty champagne bottles that are now on display in the Members' Room, was "rediscovered" recently during renovation work in the Ladies' Dressing Room area.

and although by late 1919 most members had resumed their membership and subscription income was coming in, there was a formidable mountain still to be climbed before the Club could achieve a stable financial basis. Fortunately, the Club's management was equal to the task, and through its dedication and commitment over the next several years and with Colonel Du Pre's ever present financial support, success was gradually achieved.

The Directors

Being an incorporated company, control and management were the responsibility of the directors of whom the Articles provided that there were to be not less than two and not more than five. When the company was formed in 1913, there were three directors, Colonel Du Pre, Charles Du Pre and Montrose Cloete. The Colonel, of course, was Chairman of the Board and remained so until his death in 1946.

In the thrty-five years from its incorporation in 1913 until it became a members' Club in 1948, there were only eight other directors in addition to Colonel Du Pre. These were Robert Caird (1920), Lord Churston (1933), Professor L. S. Dudgeon (1933), Sir Alexander Murray (1938), Arthur O'Bryen-Taylor (1938), Peter Case (1942), Leonard Padfield (1944) and George Langley-Taylor (1946). Although they are mentioned elsewhere, a brief note on the following may be of interest:

Robert Henryson Caird, the second son of Sir James Caird of Kirkudbrightshire, spent several years in the sheep farming industry in Australia, returning to England in 1879 where his knowledge and experience of Australia eventually led to his holding Board positions in commercial companies. He was the Du Pre family's banker and was elected a director of the Beaconsfield club in 1920. His obituary in *The Times* in May 1934, noted that "he was a keen sportsman winning many golf cups."

Richard Francis Yarde-Buller, the fourth Baron Churston, married Colonel Du Pre's daughter, Elizabeth, in 1933 and was elected a director of the club in the same year. They had one son and one daughter but, unfortunately, the marriage was dissolved in 1943 and the Board minutes for 6th November that same year record "with the greatest regret" Lord Churston's resignation as a director. Elizabeth died in 1951 and he died in 1991 at the age of eighty-one.

Leonard Stanley Dudgeon, CMG, CBE, FRCP, was Professor of Pathology at the University of London and Director of Bacteriology and Pathology at St Thomas' Hospital. He served in the First World War and was mentioned in despatches three times. Golf is stated as his recreation in *Who was Who?* and he became a member of Beaconsfield in July 1920, although the club secretary had been corresponding with him about playing at Beaconsfield since the previous August. He served on the Committee and was elected a director of the club in 1933 and remained a director until his death five years later.

Sir Alexander Robertson Murray, KCIE, CBE, was born in 1872 and spent much of his life in India, where he was extensively involved in industry and commerce and was Governor of the Imperial Bank of India from 1922 to 1927. He returned to England the next year and eventually became a director of Lloyds Bank. Sir Alexander joined the club in the early 1930s, became a director in 1938 and ten years later became the first President of the then newly formed members' club. Throughout this time, he was one of the most active members of the club and, not surprisingly, it was he who became Chairman of the Board on the death of Colonel Du Pre in 1946. He represented the members throughout the ensuing negotiations for the purchase of the clubhouse and was made a Life Member of the club in 1950.

Although meetings of the Board usually took place at the clubhouse, they were occasionally held either at Wilton Park or at Montrose Cloete's London house at 52, Berkeley Square.

The General Committee

By 1919 at the latest, rules of the Club had been established by the directors and, in accordance with those rules, a General Committee had been appointed by the Board to attend to the day- to-day running of the Club so that there was a two tier system not unlike that in proprietary golf clubs today. This General Committee, whose members were nominated annually by the directors rather than elected by the members, met about eight times a year and had power and authority, "with the assent of the directors who are *ex officio* Members of the Committee", to manage the Club's affairs and to appoint sub-committees from among their number.

From its beginning, the Club's year had always been from 1st June to 31st May and, according to the rules, it was the responsibility of the new Committee to elect a captain at its first meeting in each year. The 1932 Rules, presumably following previous precedent, provided that, in the absence of the president, the captain was to preside at meetings of the General Committee.

The Presidents

Although there is no mention of the position of president in the Articles of the 1913 company, by the time of the opening exhibition match in July 1914, a president, Lord Desborough, had been appointed and he was present on that occasion. Even though the president had, or came to have, the right by virtue of the rules of the Club to preside over meetings of the Committee, in practice he does not appear to have attended its meetings. In fact, until the Club became a members' Club in 1948, the presidents seem to have played little or no role in the management or running of the Club – which is not surprising given the presence of Colonel Du Pre himself on both the Board and the General Committee. The names of the presidents during these years need only to be listed to show the calibre of person whom the Colonel and the other directors invited to occupy that position and thereby give added prestige to the Club:

–1923 Lord Desborough

It is probable, but not certain, that Lord Desborough was President when the club opened in 1914. He was one of the Grenfell family, another of whose members, Pascoe Grenfell, was a tenant of Wilton Park at the end of the nineteenth century.

1923–1933 Lord Burnham.

1933–1947 Lord Lewisham (later the Earl of Dartmouth). Lord Lewisham was Lord Great Chamberlain of England from 1928 to 1936 when he became the Earl of Dartmouth.

Viscount Lewisham driving at the 1st in the match against the Lady Golfers Club in 1920.

The Secretaries

Captain Pellew was the first secretary of the Club, but little is known about him except that he was a nephew of Colonel Du Pre and was an executor of the Colonel's will. During Pellew's absence on military service during the First World War, a member, Humphrey Roberts, acted as secretary and, as from May 1919, George Langley-Taylor (see below) appears as assistant secretary. Roberts tendered his resignation as from 30th August 1919 and Langley-Taylor continued on his own until Pellew returned in the November. For some undisclosed reason, no sooner had Pellew returned to the Club than he resigned his post and Langley-Taylor was appointed acting secretary in December 1919, and continued as such until 1922.

Sir George Langley-Taylor, FRIBA, FRICS, FRGS was land agent for the Wilton Park estate and it was in that capacity that, over the years, he was Colonel Du Pre's right-hand man on matters relating to the course and the clubhouse and his name frequently appears in the minutes of both the Board and the Committee. On Colonel Du Pre's death, he was elected a director of the Club. Having been very much involved in the activities of the Council for the Preservation of Rural England and of several other bodies involved in the Green Belt, architecture and rural preservation generally, he received a knighthood in 1964 just before he died.

Major G. Sarel was appointed secretary as from 1st January 1922, and a few months later, as was customary in the case of secretaries, he was made an Honorary Member of the Club. As well as being a scratch golfer, he was well known as a former Sussex county cricketer and played cricket for the Beaconsfield Cricket Club who, in the 1924 season, submitted his name for Buckinghamshire county trials as a batsman.

Being the scratch golfer that he was, Sarel played regularly in club matches and competitions and started the 1924 season in great form. In April, he was fourth in the Monthly Spoon and he led the qualifiers for the Beaconsfield Challenge Bowl with a 75 gross; the following month, he won the Captain's Cup and in June he was sixth in the Bogey Sweep and second in the Medal Sweep. Unfortunately for Major Sarel, these successes did not go down too well within the Club for at the end of June the Committee decided that the secretary of the Club should no longer be eligible to play in club competitions. However, two weeks later, as if by way of recompense or perhaps from a feeling of remorse, the Committee increased his salary by £50 per annum – and he continued to play for the Club in team matches.

Unfortunately Sarel suffered periods of illness that necessitated hospitalisation from time to time but, despite this, he remained secretary until in 1928 he tendered his resignation. "Given that he has been offered the Secretaryship of the Berkshire Golf Club" the Committee decided to accept his resignation.

Lt. Colonel R. C. Weddell was the next secretary. Nothing much is known about his tenure of office, but there is something rather strange about his departure nine years later in February 1937. It is minuted that his resignation was "accepted with immediate effect" and, despite the fact that he had been with the Club for almost a decade, no customary vote of appreciation is recorded. Moreover, the minutes intriguingly record that an agreement was reached by the directors that "no official notice should be put up as to the reason for Lt. Colonel Weddell's resignation". What had happened remains a mystery.

Advertisements for a replacement were placed in *The Times*, the *Daily Telegraph* and *Golf Illustrated* and no less than 106 applications were received. Nevertheless, a decision was made quickly and barely a month had elapsed before Major H. O. Sutherland was appointed to the position in March 1937. His salary was to be £400 per month, there was to be three months' notice on either side, and "the secretary's lunch and tea to be provided by the Club". The following month he was awarded a handicap of 14 which was progressively reduced over the next eighteen months to 9; these reductions

The clubhouse in 1925

prompt speculation as to whether they were based on his general form or whether the decision about secretaries not playing in competitions had by then been reversed. On 31st August 1939, Colonel Sutherland was required to report for military service.

Membership

The return of members from First World War service progressively increased over the months following the end of the war so that by October 1919, the membership of the Club had reached nearly 400. At that time, the annual subscription for Full membership for men was seven guineas and five guineas for ladies. As a means of attracting new members, the entrance fee requirement for men, though not for ladies, was suspended for several of the early years. Subscription rates were increased remarkably little over the next twenty years so that by 1939 they were still only ten guineas and eight guineas respectively and the entrance fee for both men and women was ten guineas.

Former members of the Wilton Park Club who had continued straightaway as members of the new Beaconsfield Club had always been entitled to a reduced subscription and, even as late as 1939, twenty-five years after its demise, a reduction of three guineas in the full subscription for such male and female members was still being granted. However, this reduction did not apply to those who had been members of the Wilton Park Club, but who had not joined the Beaconsfield Club straightaway. Thus, when Kenrick Dickinson, who had been a member of the Wilton Park Club, joined the Beaconsfield Club in 1919, he had to pay the full subscription of seven guineas – but at least the entrance fee was waived. The same approach was taken in the case of a Mrs. McNair when, in 1938, she sought to "re-join" the Club "on the old subscription".

Golf in this period between the wars and especially in the home counties was still very much a game for the gentry and senior military figures, and the membership of the Beaconsfield Club very much reflected that situation. A list of the names of those elected to membership in the early years after the First World War reads like extracts from *Burke's Peerage*, the *Army and Navy Lists* and *Who's Who* – names such as Sir Crispin English, KCMG, Lt. General Sir William Pulleney, Colonel the Hon. W. A. W. Lawson, Vice-Admiral C. S. Hickley, MVO, Vice-Admiral Tudor, Lord Newton, Rt. Hon. Sir Plunkett Barton PC, Lady Catto, His Excellency Aly Cherky Pasha, J. MacNeal, Laird of Losset, Lady Dawson of Penn and so on and so on.

Among these distinguished members was another member distinguished in the world of cricket, namely Lt. Colonel the Hon. F.S. Jackson who was at one time captain of Yorkshire and England and was president of the MCC in 1931. He had a handicap of plus 2 at Beaconsfield in 1920.

The procedure for the election of members in the very early days of the Club is not known, but quite soon it became one of the responsibilities of the General Committee. There seems to have been no Membership Sub-committee, but by 1932 if not at an earlier date, the Club rule dealing with the admission of members included the ominous sentence, "One black ball shall exclude." These words remained in the rules until the Club became a members' Club in 1948 when there was a significant relaxation with the words being changed to "… and two black balls shall exclude". This element of the membership admission procedure has, of course, long since been changed.

Some members had the luxury of being able to journey to the Club by car and those fortunate enough to have chauffeurs were "requested" by the secretary to send them to the Three Horse Shoes at Seer Green, where the charge for lunch was 3s.

For those members who lived in London, and in these early days there were many, the customary way of getting to the Club was by rail rather than by road. However, although the station was most conveniently situated, as Darwin described it "within a putt of the clubhouse", problems soon arose. Too few trains to and from London stopped at Seer Green and this presented a real threat to the membership of the Club. Denham Golf Club was similarly affected and so, in October 1919, the two clubs agreed to write to the General Managers of both the Great Western Railway and the Great Central Railway to complain about the service to their respective stations. Langley-Taylor wrote on behalf of Beaconsfield to complain that his members could not get to the Club before 11.19 a.m. and he went on to say:

> This is a serious matter because members prefer to play on a course where a full round can be played before lunch.
>
> Again, on Sundays, members are unable to get a full day at the club because there is no train up to Town between 3.37 p.m. and 6.43 p.m.
>
> If you could arrange for (a) a train on weekdays to arrive from Town between 10 a.m. and 10.30 a.m. and (b) a train on Sundays to leave here for Town about 5 p.m., my Committee would much appreciate your consideration.
>
> The membership of this Club is nearly 400 and between this Club and Denham Golf Club the alterations should bring a considerable increase in passenger traffic.

Neither railway company responded in a positive way and so, "as promised", Langley-Taylor brought the matter to the attention of Lt. Colonel the Hon. J. S. Jackson MP "in the hope that you may be able to influence the companies to meet us in this matter". A measure of success appears to have followed for in November Langley-Taylor was able to write to Sir Sam Fay, who was general manager of the Great Western and Great Central Railway Joint Committee, who lived at Gerrards Cross and who happened to be a member at Beaconsfield at the time, to thank him for arranging for the 5.06 p.m. Sunday High Wycombe to Marylebone express to stop at Seer Green. He also had occasion the following month to thank Sir Sam for arranging for the 9.30 a.m. train from Marylebone to stop at Seer Green on the previous Friday and Saturday. This success led to the Committee's considering a suggestion at its next meeting that the porter at Seer Green should be asked to let the Club know when the 5.06 p.m. Sunday train had left High Wycombe. At first, the Committee did not agree with the suggestion – but some two meetings later it did agree to purchase a handbell for the station porter to ring in order to notify golfers in the clubhouse when the train for London was approaching Seer Green. The next year, the Committee received a letter from the railway company proposing "the erection of an electric bell in the Clubhouse at a cost of £4 with an annual maintenance cost of £1" and the Committee agreed to accept the proposal. This "bell contract" with GWR lasted until 1949 when the Board agreed to British Rail's proposal to terminate it.

The Caricatures

In 1928, Montrose Cloete commissioned a cartoonist, H. F. Crowther-Smith, to sketch several of the directors and Committee members and the framed montage of these caricatures that he presented to the Club still hangs in the Members' Room. On the reverse side is written:

Beaconsfield Golf Club

Beaconsfield Golf Club is situated in the beautifully wooded Park on the estate of Lt. Colonel Du Pre. The Clubhouse, a fine red-brick, mullioned structure built in 1914, is – as Bernard Darwin expresses it – within a putt of the Station.

The course, because of its high elevation, enjoys comparative immunity from the excessive rain-fall of the past months. Lt. Colonel Du Pre, Mr. Montrose Cloete and Mr. Robert H. Caird are Directors of the Club.

Presented by Montrose Cloete, April 1928

A montage of caricatures drawn in 1937 by "Mel" of *The Tatler* magazine is also on display in the Members' Room.

Bar and Catering

In the early days, the bar and catering services were invariably provided by a steward whose wife was the cook. The basis of the arrangement was that the Club fixed the prices and the standard of meals and it was for the steward and his wife to provide the services accordingly. It was on this basis that Mr. and Mrs. Dale were employed in 1920 and all went well until the Committee introduced a new approach to the catering arrangements whereby, under the general supervision of the House Committee and subject to the Committee setting the prices of meals, responsibility for the catering was to be entirely in the hands of the steward. He was, however, given to understand that "if he found it impossible to run the catering at a profit, he could approach the Committee with a view to reverting to the old system". The Committee then fixed the price of meals as follows:

Lunch	3s.6d.
Weekday lunch (ladies only)	2s.6d.
Teas	1s., 9d. and 6d.

Alas, this new arrangement proved highly unsatisfactory for the Dales, so much so that at the end of that year, Colonel Du Pre himself became very much aware of the problem that this new system was causing them. He therefore wrote to Montrose Cloete to tell him that he had spoken to Sarel, the secretary, about Dale whose catering figures for the first eleven months of the year showed that he had made a loss of £120 – "almost the amount of his salary". Colonel Du Pre went on in his letter to say, "Dale

58

The montage of caricatures presented by Montrose Cloet, 1928

Caricatures by "Mel" of The Tatler, *1937*

The dining room, 1925

has been very good about it and has made no direct claims, but Sarel and I agree that something must be done at once." When Dale himself was asked what he thought should be done, he said that, with a salary increase of £10 per month together with his increased experience and a larger attendance, he would be able to see his way through. The directors agreed to the increase and initially the problem seemed to have been resolved, but the Dales were not happy with the arrangement, tendered their resignations and left the Club in 1924.

Arthur Coxall and his wife replaced the Dales and stayed at the Club for fourteen years. They proved to be very satisfactory and all went well until a difference of opinion on meal pricing arose that culminated in Coxall being threatened with losing his job. In November 1935 the Committee had decided that at weekends a cold meat or pie luncheon followed by cheese and biscuits should be available for 2s.6d. Coxall was called to the Committee meeting to be given this information and then told to go away and discuss the matter with his wife. Coxall returned to the meeting to say that it was impossible to put on such a meal for that price whereupon it appears that Colonel Du Pre firmly retorted that the Committee was insistent and that if he could not do it "other arrangements would be made". Being understandably concerned for their jobs, the Coxalls had a re-think and at the next meeting of the Committee Coxall presented alternative menu suggestions for weekend lunches that he and his wife were prepared to put on and, "after full discussion", the Committee chose the following menu:

Hot lunch	3s.6d.
Cold meat lunch with salad, pickles, cheese and biscuits	2s.6d.
Cold meat lunch with hot vegetables, sweet or cheese and biscuits	2s.6d.

In addition, the Committee agreed that, at weekends, the steward could charge 1s. for second helpings of cold lunches.

Coxall tendered his resignation in May 1938 saying in his letter of resignation that he regarded it as "his duty to accept a position carrying a higher salary". In appreciation of the fourteen years good service that the Coxalls had given to the Club, a donation list was opened with an upper limit of 5s. per member. Even so, the amount collected enabled the Club to present them with a tea tray chosen by the Coxalls and a cheque for £18.19s.0d. which was the balance of the fund. In an issue of *Golf Illustrated* ten years later it was reported that Arthur Coxall had recently retired as steward at Swinley Forest because of ill-health. At that time, one of his brothers was the steward at Royal Mid-Surrey and another brother had at one time been steward at Muirfield.

The following month, Mr. and Mrs. Jack Cooper were appointed steward and stewardess on terms that the steward was to be entirely responsible for catering and that he would be entitled to 80% of any profit on the catering account and bear twenty percent of any loss. Moreover, he was to be responsible for the provision of the necessary catering staff, but the Club would make a contribution of £200 towards their wages.

Although the Coopers did not leave the Club until ten years later, Jack had scarcely settled into his new position when, like others on the Club staff, he was called up for military service.

While the steward's responsibilities included the bar generally, bar prices remained a matter for the General Committee on the recommendation of the House Committee. Over the years, prices fluctuated – down as well as up. For example, in January 1921, the prices of whiskey and gin were increased to "10d for half a noggin and 1s.8d. for a noggin" – a term that probably meant a small measure or "nip", for a noggin is usually understood to be a quarter of a pint and it seems scarcely credible that the Club would have served such a measure at such a price. For brandy, prices were increased to 1s.3d. and 2s.6d. respectively. Two years later, following the secretary's report that bar sales for the six months to the end of November 1923 showed a profit of £320.10s.7d., the Committee agreed certain price reductions:

Dow's 1908 Port (per bottle)	from 18s. to 16s.
Taylor's 1908 Port (per bottle)	from 9s. to 8s.6d.
Large whiskey or gin	to be 1s.7d

It was in connection not so much with bar sales as with bar purchases that tragedy befell the Club in May 1927 when "a jar containing six gallons of whiskey during transit from the station to the clubhouse" was dropped and broken. In reporting this tragedy to the Board, the secretary said that he had received a letter from the carriers, Messrs H. Roberts & Co., stating that they were not legally liable for the loss, but that they were agreeable to making a contribution. The directors forwarded the matter to the Club's solicitors for their opinion, but sadly there is no record as to the outcome. Nonetheless, it must have been an unusual pleasure for several days after the disaster to walk across the members' car park and breathe the wholesome air of the glens.

The Club was, of course, still a proprietary club and, at a Committee meeting in 1934, Sir James Donald expressed the view that, for the purposes of the licensing laws, the Club probably now needed to have a Wine Committee appointed by the members. Having made enquiries, the secretary reported to the Board that, while all clubs were required to register with their local court if intoxicating liquor was habitually supplied to members, if the Club was a proprietary club, a separate and additional liquor licence was also necessary. This was because, unlike the position in a members' club, the members of a proprietary club did not own the liquor stock or, indeed, any of the Club's property. However, in order to avoid the need for a proprietary club to hold this separate liquor licence, a device had been developed whereby control of the purchase and sale of liquor was nominally vested in a committee appointed by the members of the Club and it was this committee that technically made the sale to fellow members. The Board therefore adopted this device, and a Wine Committee was established and continued in existence even after the members' Club was formed, but then it was just a committee responsible for the bar and bar prices.

Following a recommendation of the Club's auditors, a separate bank account was opened in the name of the Wine Committee so as to facilitate the Club "recovering" the profit made on bar sales by imposing a monthly charge on the Wine Committee in respect of "the rent of the bar and the provision of other services". Initially, this monthly charge was £20 but by 1939 it had reached £40.

The Staff Christmas Fund

It is a tradition and rule at most clubs that members do not give gratuities to staff, but that they show their appreciation by donating to a staff Christmas Fund. This has been the case at Beaconsfield from the early days and remains so today. The earliest surviving copy of the "Xmas Fund List" showing the amount collected and its distribution, is the one for 1933.

This list is particularly interesting, not only because its shows the full complement of the Club's indoor and outdoor staff at the time (a head greenkeeper and no less than nine "groundsmen"), but also because it shows that the professional at the time, Percy Alliss, was included in the distribution. This is rather odd because in 1924 the Committee had decided that, since the professional was not an employee of the Club, he should not participate in the distribution of the Christmas Fund. However, by 1933, the Committee had clearly had a change of mind. The following year, Percy Alliss sought permission to put up a Christmas Fund List in his shop for the benefit of his assistants, but the Committee refused to sanction this, pointing out that his share of the Club's Christmas Fund was intended to cover his assistants as well as himself.

Clubhouse Alterations

Although the clubhouse was only five years old, already by 1919 consideration was being given to alterations. The clubhouse architect, Stanley Hamp, was asked to prepare sketches for extending the Men's dressing room "which was now far too small" and to give his views as to whether it would be possible to provide two or three bedrooms and a bathroom over such extension for the use of directors and whether it would be possible to provide further staff accommodation. It was in this connection that, on 20th May 1919, the Club secretary, Langley-Taylor, wrote to the Surveyor at the Amersham Rural District Council to say that he would be calling on him the next day to discuss the plans for the proposed alterations, and concluded his letter with the words, "I am leaving here tomorrow at 2 p.m. in a trap and so should reach you at 3 p.m." In the event, these particular proposals did not materialise, although a cellar was constructed later that year.

The Golf Illustrated Gold Vase, one the most prestigious amateur tournaments, was played at Beaconsfield in 1927 and the magazine's report of the event includes a photograph of the clubhouse taken from the 18th green. Not only does this photograph show the complete set of the dominant chimney stacks that were a principal feature of the new clubhouse, but it also shows that the staff accommodation extension between the main building and the caddie-master's house had not then been built.

The following year the Club invited quotations for a variety of "necessary alterations and additions" to the clubhouse and, while it is not known for certain what these were, it is very probable that they related to the building of the staff accommodation extension on the east wing towards the caddie-master's house. Recently a copy of the costed quotation submitted for building works by Messrs Francis Newton of Hitchin has come into the Club's possession and this indicates that work to the south and east wings was certainly included. In the event, the directors approved the lower quotation of £1,500 submitted by Messrs Trickey and it was recorded that "Colonel Du Pre is willing to put up the money for the scheme". At the AGM the following year, it was reported that the rebuilding and alterations had been satisfactorily completed and that the cost had been paid out of income "with expenses and wages having been cut and having waived interest payment on debentures".

The architect for these works was Walter Sarel of Eaton Square, London, and given the unusual surname, it is probably safe to assume that he was related to the Major Sarel who was the Club secretary from 1922 until 1928.

The question of installing shower baths was first mooted in 1924, but it was not until 1937 that the Committee eventually accepted a quotation of £52.10s.0d. from Messrs. Y. J. Lovell for the installation of two combination shower/foot baths in the Men's changing room and a quotation of £12.15s.0d. for a footbath in the Ladies Dressing Room. An additional sum, "not to exceed £12.5s.", was approved to screen off part of the Ladies Room. In fact, the improvements to the Ladies Dressing Room exceeded the estimate by £2 but, "after due consideration", the Committee generously authorised the additional expenditure.

Chapter Seven

The Golfing Scene
1919 to 1939

The Second Opening Exhibition Match

GOLFING ACTIVITIES at the new Club began to pick up with the gradual return of members and staff from war service. The outbreak of war had followed so hard upon the opening exhibition match in 1914 that an altogether fresh start was needed and, as if to replicate on an even grander scale the original opening of the new course, the Committee decided in January 1920, to stage a second exhibition match. The relevant minute read simply:

> 19. The Secretary was instructed to write to the following professionals to arrange a suitable day for a competition to be played on the Course Viz:—
>
> Mitchell - Duncan - & Vardon & Braid
>
> *Mortimer Coats*
> *Chairman 6 Jan 1920*

These four professionals were among the most famous golfers in the country at the time. Vardon's successes in the Open have already been mentioned in a previous Chapter. James Braid had won the Open five times between 1901 and 1910 and George Duncan won it in 1920. Abe Mitchell had won several tournaments, but had never managed to win the Open although he led Duncan by thirteen shots after two rounds in 1920.

James Braid

Harry Vardon

Abe Mitchell

George Duncan

Dutifully, the secretary wrote to Harry Vardon, then the professional at South Herts, to James Braid at Walton Heath, to Abe Mitchell at Sonning on Thames and to George Duncan at Hangar Hill and, eventually, Saturday 27th March was chosen as the date for the match. The terms for each professional were agreed at "ten guineas for the day, plus expenses". The Committee decided that there should be no admission charge for the public and no limit on the number of spectators.

There is no doubt that this exhibition match was designed to re-establish Beaconsfield firmly and squarely on the golfing map and, therefore, appropriate publicity was essential. To this end and on the suggestion of a Mr. Shilcock, a member at Beaconsfield, the secretary wrote in February to the Topical Press Agency in London to draw their attention to the exhibition match on the 27th March, and also to the Lloyds' Spring Meeting that was to be held at Beaconsfield on the 9th March. He invited the Agency to send a representative down to take photographs and asked whether they could "guarantee the pictures appearing in all the important daily, weekly and monthly papers". A similar letter was also written to George Greenwood, golf correspondent of the *Daily Telegraph*, asking if he would write an article on the two fixtures and inviting him to visit Beaconsfield on either or both of the dates or at any time.

In the exhibition match itself, Vardon lost to Braid at the 17th in one of the morning singles matches while, in the other singles match, Mitchell beat Duncan by one hole. In the afternoon fourball, the younger pairing of Mitchell and Duncan beat their elders by 2 and 1. The only details about the matches that have been discovered are that Vardon bunkered his tee shot at the 5th and that "Mitchell hit a tree at the 6th with his tee shot, but only because he was attempting to make a Herculean straight line carry at the dog-leg hole" (*The Car* magazine for January 1921).

The Club's prestige must have been enhanced even further when in 1927 The Golf Illustrated Gold Vase, was played at Beaconsfield and extensively reported in the magazine's issue for 15th April. The thirty-six hole stroke play event brought together many of the great names of amateur golf at the time and led to an absorbing tussle at the end between two Walker Cup players, Roger Wethered and Cyril Tolley, with the former's score of 151 being good enough to win by one stroke. The Club's secretary, Major Sarel, participated and, given the rainswept conditions of the day, did remarkably well in returning a score of 165.

Club Competitions

The Sir John Aird Cup, which had been presented to the Wilton Park Club back in 1909, continued to played for and several of the trophies that are still played for today were presented in these early years. These included:[†]

The Beaconsfield Challenge Bowl presented by local members in 1920.

The Lewis Pawle Cup presented by Lewis S. Pawle in 1920.

The Grange Cup presented by J. H. Guy in 1921.

The Wilton Park Challenge Cup presented by Colonel Du Pre in 1921.
[The first winners of this mixed foursome cup were the celebrated Miss Cecil Leitch and Mr. W. E. Broomfield who beat Mrs. Drage and Mr. P. C. Raffety by 6 and 4 – a match reported in the *Evening Standard* on 22nd March 1921.]

The Montrose Cloete Cup presented by Montrose Cloete in 1929.

The Mr. Broomfield referred to above as partnering Miss Cecil Leitch in winning the Wilton Park Challenge Cup in 1921, had become a member of the Club only the previous year. He had a handicap of 6 and he resigned his membership two years later. However, while he was a member, he presented a cup to the Club and a minute of a Committee meeting held in April 1921 records that "A qualifying round for Mr. Broomfield's cup will be played on Saturday 7th May." The Raffety account asserts that this is the same cup that "we have for some reason for a long time been wrongly calling the Bloomfield". It has not yet been possible to establish definitively whether the Bloomfield cup and the Broomfield cup are in fact one and the same, but the probability is that they are. Today, the Bloomfield Cup[††] is a men's foursomes knockout competition, but the Club's Fixture List for 1938 indicates that, at that time, the Broomfield cup was preceded by a qualifying medal round: "Men's Foursomes Competition under handicap for Cup presented by W. E. Broomfield (eight to qualify)".

In April 1922 the R&A wrote to all golf clubs inviting subscriptions to defray the cost of staging the Amateur and Open Championships and also asking clubs to post a subscription list on their notice boards inviting donations from members towards the cost of sending a team of amateurs to America. That team was, of course, to be the first Walker Cup team and was to play the American team at Long Island, NY later that year. As regards defraying the cost of the championships, the Committee decided to send a donation of one guinea, but as regards support for a team to go to America, the Committee decided that "it was not in the interest of Amateur golf to post a subscription list in the Clubhouse" and no contribution was sent.

[†]The ladies' competitions in the early years are mentioned in the Chapter on the Ladies' Section.
[††]The honours board for the Bloomfield Cup only starts at 1965, but competition for the Cup dates back to 1921.

The Club Championship

The thirty-six hole Club Championship stroke play competition was instituted in 1936 and the Committee selected the championship trophy from a selection of cups and bowls made available at the Club by Waring & Gillow of Tottenham Court Road. The championship, for which entries were restricted to those with handicaps of 6 and under, was held for the first time on Saturday 2nd May that year and the winner was Ken Braddon. Ken was a scratch golfer for many years and a very active member of the Club, as indeed was his wife, both before and after the war. He was captain of the Club in 1968 and for several years during the 1970s was the organiser of junior golf at the Club. Ken went on to win the Club Championship for the next two years and for a total of six times altogether – an achievement equalled by his son Richard, who is now secretary at Pannal Golf Club. That achievement has only been exceeded by Ian Wheater who won the Club Championship ten consecutive times from 1972 to 1981.

There are many stories about Ken Braddon, who was something of a flamboyant character, as well befitted an advertising man. One of the stories concerns his return from competing in the English Amateur Championship at Hollinwell, Nottinghamshire, sometime in the 1930s. He caught *The Master Cutler* from Sheffield and it so happened on that particular day that this express train to London made a totally unscheduled stop at Seer Green where Ken alighted. Ken always said that it was the best half-a-crown he had ever spent.

Club Matches

Matches against neighbouring clubs and against golfing societies soon began to find their way into the fixture list with the first inter-club match being against Denham on 19th May 1920. It was an away match and Denham won the morning singles by 7 matches to 2 and the afternoon foursomes by 3 matches to 2. In the return match at Beaconsfield in November, Beaconsfield faired marginally better, only losing the singles by 6 matches to 2; the foursomes were again lost by the same margin. Colonel Du Pre himself played in both of these opening matches, winning his away foursomes and halving his home singles. Despite the results in these initial matches, the annual fixtures with Denham have continued ever since except for the war years and are as popular with members today as they have always been.

Other men's team matches and then ladies' team matches against Berkhamsted, Ellesborough, Flackwell Heath and other local clubs were arranged soon afterwards. For obvious reasons, men's matches were usually arranged for weekends, but it is clear that they were frowned upon by many of the members who highly valued their social weekend games. The matter

*Mr. and Mrs. P. C. Harvey (Beaconsfield) playing Mrs. Rowden and Major Swan (Stoke Poges)
in a mixed team match at Beaconsfield, 1921*

came to a head in October 1921 when members became aware that Saturday
fixtures had been arranged with the Army Golfing Society, the Navy Golfing
Society and Oxford and Cambridge Universities. Because of the strong
concerns expressed, men's team matches were subsequently often played on
a Wednesday even though it appears to have been difficult to raise a team to
play in midweek matches.

Mixed team matches were also arranged as early as 1921. The earliest for
which records exist is the match against Stoke Poges at Beaconsfield on 19th
November 1924. That match comprised sixteen singles in the morning,
which Beaconsfield lost, and eight foursomes in the afternoon which
Beaconsfield won. In the return match the following February played over
the "Links of the Stoke Poges Golf Club", Beaconsfield lost the morning
singles by 12 1/2 matches to 3 1/2 and were, perhaps, somewhat fortunate that
"Rain prevented any play in the afternoon foursomes."

The early club matches against Golfing Societies included those against
the Household Brigade, the Brigade of Guards, the Ranelagh Club, the
Army Golfing Society and the Stage Golfing Society. In July 1921, there
was even a match against a team of American cricketers who were touring
the UK that year.

The first match against the Stage Golfing Society was played on 3rd
October 1920, with the astonishing number of forty players each. The Stage

George Langley-Taylor, secretary, in conversation with Ernest Graham, secretary of the Stage Golfing Society, 1920

Golfing Society won by 18 matches to 14 with 8 halved. According to the report of the match in the *Bucks Herald*, after the match "Dinner was served in the Golf-house, 214 guests enjoying a capital repast". Unless 214 was a misprint, both the Dining Room and the Lounge would have had to be used. Following the speeches, the Society provided "an excellent concert". Two months later, there was another match against the Stage Golfing Society, but on this occasion it was only nine-a-side and again the Society won the match. Colonel Du Pre played against Leslie Henson, a very famous comedian of the time and, according to one of his daughters, when the Colonel got home after the match and was asked how he had got on, he replied that he had lost by 2 and 1 but would have won easily if the young comedian he was playing against had not made him laugh all the way round. Implausible as that excuse may appear, it probably has more than a grain of truth in it because, just as the Colonel had his idiosyncratic croquet style of putting, so Leslie Henson had his own peculiarities on the green. The match between these two players moved George Greenwood, the *Daily Telegraph* reporter, to write in his account of the match on 11th December:

> It is not often, however, that one meets two players in a match who are eccentric in their respective styles. Yesterday, however, at Beaconsfield I received an unmistakable shock.

And he went on to describe Leslie Henson's style in these words:

> Both hands were brought into operation for the long putts and only one for the little ones … but when he thrust his left hand into his pocket and putted solely with his right hand he contrived to miss more than he holed … Altogether it was a day of ghastly tragedies on the green.

In 1921, the secretary of Burnham Beeches wrote to six of the local clubs to propose that they hold an inter-club foursomes match in which each club would be represented by the professional and an amateur. The professionals were to play off scratch and each club team was to have a handicap equal to half the amateur's handicap. In August, the Beaconsfield secretary, Langley-

Taylor, responded to the proposal indicating that the Club was pleased to participate, "it being understood that the arrangement is for one year only and will be reviewed yearly". There are no Beaconsfield records as to whether this match ever took place or was repeated but, later that same year, Langley-Taylor wrote to the secretary of the Handicap Committee of the R&A in connection with the proposed match. Having explained the proposal, he pointed out that one of the amateurs taking part had a handicap of plus 4, and therefore he would like to know what handicap his team should have plus 2 or plus 8? There is no record of the response that was received, but undoubtedly the amateur that Langley-Taylor had in mind was Reymond H. De Montmorency, about whom more is written in Chapter Fourteen.

Golfing Societies

Because of the quality of the clubhouse and the course and the ease of access by rail, many golfing societies based in London chose to hold their meetings in the 1920s and 1930s at Beaconsfield. Among these societies were the Ministry of Health Golfing Society, the Ladies Medical Golfing Society, the Garrick Golfing Society, St Stephens Golfing Society, the Air Ministry Golfing Society, the R.A.M.C. Golfing Society and Lloyds Golfing Society.

One of the first societies to hold a meeting on the new Beaconsfield course was the Advertisers' Golfing Society and, in writing to confirm the date of the fixture as being 10th July 1919, the Beaconsfield secretary responded to the Society's request for caddies to be available by saying, "… it is no easy matter to get fifty or sixty caddies here on a week-day so as many of your members as possible should bring caddies with them".

Some golfing societies sought and were granted "affiliation" to the club which meant that, in return for an agreed annual fee, their members could play at Beaconsfield on weekdays free of charge, but could only play at weekends and on public holidays on payment of a green fee. The Stage Golfing Society was one of the first such affiliated societies.

The Lady Golfers' Club, based in London, was another organisation that was "affiliated" to Beaconsfield, also in 1920, and this affiliation continued until 1947. It enabled the Club to become members of the Buckinghamshire County Lady Golfing Association. The Lady Golfers' Club held its Annual Meetings and played all or most of its competitions and matches at Beaconsfield right up to the outbreak of war. There was also an annual match against the Beaconsfield men's team, the first of which was a twenty-a-side singles and foursomes match played in 1920. On that occasion the ladies were captained by the celebrated Miss Cecil Leitch, a scratch player who was four times British Ladies champion and a regular member of the English Ladies team from 1910 to 1928. The Club's team was captained by

Mr. Reymond Hervey De Montmorency and Miss Cecil Leitch, respective captains of Beaconsfield and the Lady Golfers Club in the match at Beaconsfield, 1921

Reymond H. de Montmorency who, playing off plus 3 led his team to a substantial win by 21½ matches to 8½. It was probably because of this resounding win that in the match the following year each of the ladies was allowed what *The Times* golf correspondent referred to as "a sex allowance of six strokes" – and Beaconsfield lost the singles by 11 matches to nil and won the afternoon foursomes by 3 matches to 1. In 1922, both de Montmorency and Miss Leitch were made Honorary Members of the Club.

In the 1927 match against the Stage Golfing Society, Bernard Darwin (plus 1 handicap) who was by then an Honorary Member of the Club, played top in the singles against Miss Helme (3 handicap) who received no less than 9 "sex allowance" (courtesy) strokes; Darwin lost by 2 and 1.

The Professionals

James H. Jones 1914–1932

So far as is known, there was no professional golfer attached to the Wilton Park Club and therefore the distinction of being the first professional to be associated with a golf club at Beaconsfield goes to James Jones. Jones had joined the Professional Golfers' Association in 1902 and had been the professional at Bexhill Golf Club, Sussex, from 1910 until 1913 when he left to take up the position at the newly formed Beaconsfield Club.

Jones played in the opening exhibition match in July 1914, but shortly afterwards he was called to military service. There is no information as to what Jones' war service involved, but the probability is that it contributed to the ill-health that dogged him for many years afterwards. This ill-health was already apparent in July 1919 when the secretary had occasion to write to Colonel Du Pre to tell him that Dr. Parshall, one of the members of the Club with a practice in Beaconsfield, had suggested that Jones go away for a month to Frinton. In his letter seeking the Colonel's sanction to this proposal, the secretary wrote, "I understand that this is quite a usual proceeding and I think that a holiday would do Jones good: of course he has only been back here [from the war] quite a short time, but he would arrange with Woods who was his assistant before the war to look after things." The directors agreed to Jones having the month of August as his holiday.

Again in 1922 Jones was given a month's leave of absence due to illness and the following year he was given a month's leave of absence to go to the south of France for health reasons. In all, Jones remained with the Club for eighteen years and would probably have made quite a name for himself in golfing circles had he not suffered persistent poor health. He left the Club in 1932 and moved to Kington Golf Club in Herefordshire and later to Brand Hall Golf Club near Birmingham. He seems to have retired sometime during the Second World War. Recently, during his year as captain, Jim Lawson discovered and purchased a persimmon headed, hickory shafted brassie (2-wood) bearing the stamp of "J. H. Jones, Beaconsfield Golf Club". He had the club mounted and donated it to the Club and it is now displayed in the Members' Room.

It is interesting to note that from 1929 to 1931 Jones' assistant at Beaconsfield was W. J. "Bill" Cox who played in the Ryder Cup teams of 1935 and 1937 and went on to be one of the country's best known professional golfers and, perhaps, an even better known teacher of the game. Bill was born in Chalfont St Giles and was at one time professional at Gerrards Cross.

Percy Alliss 1932–1936

By the time Jones left in 1932, the Club was fast becoming one of the most prestigious clubs in the south of England and it is clear that the directors and Committee were keen to confirm that status by engaging a professional whose achievements and reputation would add to that prestige. Percy Alliss was just the sort of person they were looking for – a well established tournament player with many successes to his name both at home and abroad who had already won the German Open four times, the Italian Open and several other continental titles as well as having played in the Ryder Cup matches in 1929 and 1931. Percy had been the professional at the Wannsee Golf Club in Berlin since 1928 and it was while he was there that his son, Peter, was born. Not surprisingly, Percy Alliss was chosen to succeed Jones and he came to Beaconsfield in 1932. Later that year he published an instructional booklet entitled *Making Golf Easier* and describing himself as "The Professional at Beaconsfield Golf Club".

It is uncertain whether the Alliss family occupied the professional's house beside the 7th tee which at that time was known as The Seventh; there seems to have been no reason why they did not live there, but Peter Alliss has no recollection of doing so and believes that they lived elsewhere in Beaconsfield.

Percy Alliss had not long been with the Club when, in January 1934, the Committee had to consider "complaints from some members about his using the Clubhouse and Luncheon Room". After due consideration and having regard to the practice in many clubs at that time, the Committee decided that in future he would be allowed to use the clubhouse premises only under certain circumstances. Colonel Du Pre, who chaired that particular meeting of the Committee, agreed "to see Alliss at an early date and explain the position to him". Reporting this episode at the meeting of the Board held in April, the Colonel said that he had explained to Alliss that, in view of the fact that certain members of the Club had objected to his using the clubhouse and that certain remarks had been passed, it was thought advisable that in future he should not use the clubhouse or accept the hospitality of members. However, the Colonel said that he had made it quite clear to Alliss that there was nothing personal against him in any way and that very probably, if he remained at the Club a little longer, the question of his being made an Honorary Member would be considered.

Professor Dudgeon, a director, continued the report to the Board by saying that, despite the Colonel's explanation, Alliss himself had seen the matter in a different way and had tendered a letter of resignation. Dudgeon went on to say that, following the receipt of that letter, he had had a private discussion with Alliss who, having received Dudgeon's personal assurance that the Committee would go fully into the matter again, withdrew and destroyed the letter. After reviewing the delicate situation, the Board decided that the Committee should consider the whole matter again. Not surprisingly, at a meeting of the Committee held later that very same Saturday, Colonel Du Pre proposed and Professor Dudgeon seconded a resolution that "Percy Alliss, the professional, be made an Honorary Member of the Club" – a resolution that was carried unanimously. The tradition of appointing the club professional as an Honorary Member was thus established and so ended happily what had been a most unfortunate episode – but one that may have had a longer term effect on the relationship between Alliss and the Club.

During his time at Beaconsfield, Percy Alliss established a new professional course record of 64 and had reduced it to 62 by the time he left. He also continued to play successfully in professional tournaments both at home and abroad. In 1935, he won the Italian Open at San Remo and was again selected to play in the Ryder Cup match, this time at Ridgewood, New Jersey. It was also while he was at Beaconsfield the he took delivery of a new car which he proudly displayed on the lawn beneath what is now the secretary's office window. This must have been quite some event for, as his son Peter recalls, there were probably only three golf professionals who were grand enough to

Percy Alliss with his new car

own motor cars at that time, the other two being Henry Cotton and Arthur Havers.

Being born and bred a Yorkshireman, the call of his native county proved too strong for Alliss to resist the temptation to apply for the post of professional at the Temple Newsam Golf Club in Leeds and, being successful, he resigned his post at Beaconsfield in January 1936. The Committee recorded "a very hearty vote of thanks to Alliss for the excellent services he had rendered the Club during his office" and, at the express wish of many members, a presentation list was opened with an upper limit of 10s. per member. It is not recorded what presentation gift was purchased, but it is known that it cost £8.2s.9d. more than the amount that had been collected but that the Club made up the balance. The presentation was made to Alliss after a morning medal round between him and the newly appointed professional, Ernest Kenyon, and this was followed by a mixed foursomes competition for members in the afternoon.

Percy Alliss competed in the Open several times, but the nearest he came to winning was at Carnoustie in 1931 when he finished third. In the 1936 Open at Hoylake, he shared fifth place with Tom Green who was the professional at Burnham Beeches at that time. Successful as he was, it was always said of Percy Alliss that he would have been an even more successful golfer had he been more aggressive and ruthless but, commenting on this in his tribute to Percy Alliss in *Golf Illustrated* on the occasion of his retirement in 1967, Tom Scott said "that would not have been him – he was just not that kind of bloke".

Concluding the account of his visit to Beaconsfield in 1932, G.A. Philpot, the editor of *Tee Topics,* wrote:

> The Club is fortunate in having recently acquired the services of Percy Alliss. I heard words of commendation about him from many members; and although he has been with the Club only a few weeks, he is already an established favourite. Modest, unassuming and a great golfer, Alliss is a model professional in every sense of the term. Lucky is the Club to have such a professional; lucky is Alliss to be attached to such a Club.

E. W. H. Kenyon 1936–1948

No sooner had Percy Alliss tendered his resignation than the Club received three applications for the post. These were from E. W. H. Kenyon, who was then at West Lancs, J. Adams at Romford and J. Machie at Hunstanton. Nevertheless, the Committee decided to put these applications on hold until the post had been advertised in *Golf Illustrated* and "selected national newspapers". Eventually, after considering the applications, the list was narrowed down to Ernest "Bob" Kenyon and Jimmy Adams. Having agreed the terms that could be offered, the Committee decided that Bob Kenyon should be the first to be interviewed, and he was invited to meet Colonel Du Pre and Professor Dudgeon at Carlton House Terrace on Friday 13th March at 2 p.m. One has to wonder how many other professional golfers have been interviewed in such grand surroundings and on such an inauspicious date. Nevertheless, the interview was successful and Bob Kenyon was appointed professional on the following terms:

- rent free occupation of The Seventh
- a retainer fee of £200 per annum
- sixty-five days absence per annum for tournaments
- 5s. per round plus caddie fee if playing a single or 7s.6d. per round plus caddie fee if two or more players
- to retain at least one first class playing assistant
- lesson fees to be 4s.6d. for half an hour and 6s.6d. for one hour (charges for Seer Green House pupils to be 4s. for half an hour with Kenyon or 3s. with the first assistant)
- three months notice on either side

Having learned from experience, the Committee made it plain to Kenyon at the outset that he could go into the clubhouse only if he was invited by a member and that he was not to have meals there without the permission of the secretary or, in his absence, a member of the Committee.

Bob Kenyon driving at the 1st in an exhibition match with Percy Alliss, Bill Cox and Henry Cotton
(standing behind Bob Kenyon)

Though perhaps not quite the same class of golfer as his predecessor, Bob Kenyon was nevertheless an experienced tournament professional. He had won the South Wales Professional Championship in 1928, the Irish Open in three successive years from 1931 and, in the 1939 Open which was played at St Andrews and won by Dick Burton, he finished in twenty-ninth place jointly with Bobby Locke and Percy Alliss, who by then was the professional at Ferndown.

Following the outbreak of the Second World War, Kenyon left the Club in July 1940 and enlisted for military service and there was no professional at the Club during the war.

And the "Local Rules"

Until the Second World War, each member of the Club received a booklet entitled the "Rules of the Beaconsfield Golf Club"† setting out the constitution of the Club, membership categories, election procedures, local rules and so on. The earliest surviving copy of the Rules booklet is the one for 1932 and this sets out the bye-laws and the local rules for playing the course.

†It seems that this booklet was not continued after the war and that it was replaced by an Official Handbook which was published periodically and served more as a promotional booklet than as an information handbook for members.

However, even though Rules booklets earlier than 1932 are not now available, some of the early bye-laws and local rules can be gathered from minutes of meetings of the Committees at which they were adopted.

For example, in June 1921 a new local rule was introduced regarding balls played out of bounds onto the railway line at the 11th and 12th holes; the penalty was changed to be distance only. From this it would appear that, at that time, it was a matter for each club to decide what the penalty for out of bounds should be and reference to a book on the history of the Rules of Golf shows that this was indeed the case. Between 1909 and 1920, the Rules of Golf provided that the penalty for a ball played out of bounds was distance only, but clubs had the authority to require the addition of a penalty stroke as well if they so wished and could do so by making a local rule to that effect. However, the R&A then reversed that Rule so that, after 1920, in the absence of a club's local rule saying that it was to be distance only, the penalty for out of bounds was to be stroke and distance. Thus it was that in 1921 the Beaconsfield Committee decided to make a local rule that continued the out of bounds penalty as distance only. But that was not the end of the story for two years later the Committee abolished that local rule since when the out of bounds penalty at the 11th and 12th holes has been stroke and distance. Why these changes were made and why there was never any mention in the local rule of the out of bounds penalty applicable at the 13th specifically or, indeed, at any other hole where there was an out of bounds, remains a mystery.

In 1924 the Committee formally decided that there should not be a local rule permitting a ball to be wiped on the green, but by 1932 a different view had been taken, for local rule number 5 allowed a ball on the green to be wiped but "before the first putt only". Interestingly, in the Rules booklet three years later, this local rule had been changed to read:

> The ball may be wiped on actual cut green before the first putt only and not on the putting green as defined by the Rules of Golf.

The difference expressed in this local rule between being "on actual cut green" and "not on the putting green as defined by the Rules of Golf" is intriguing but not readily apparent.

In the 1932 booklet, bye-law number 1 (and it probably was a bye-law long before then) is very much a sign of those times: "Players without caddies shall give way to players accompanied by caddies."

In October 1935 the Committee received a letter from a member of the Club who had recently played at the Royal Wimbledon Golf Club where he had seen several local rules applicable to fourball matches and which he thought should be adopted at Beaconsfield. These rules, designed to avoid the slow play that, in those days, seems always to have been attributed to fourballs, were:

(1) If a ball be played out of bounds, the player shall take no further part in the hole.

(2) If a ball be lost, only the player and his caddie shall look for it.

(3) Under no circumstances may a player play two strokes more than his partner.

(4) No player shall putt out if his partner has won the hole.

(5) At least two caddies must be employed in any fourball match.

After due consideration, the Committee thought that these rules made good sense, agreed to adopt them and to have them printed and exhibited in the clubhouse. It is not known when these rules were abolished – or were they? It is interesting to note that as recently as January 2001 the secretary of Royal Wimbledon confirmed that the Club "still apply points (1) and (2) and sometimes points (3) and (4), but sadly economics mean that point (5) is now irrelevant".

"The Deadwood on the First" by Val Doonican

Chapter Eight

War, Peace and the End of An Era
1939 to 1946

W HEN THE First World War was declared in August 1914, the clubhouse and the course were brand new, the opening exhibition match had been played only three weeks earlier and there had been no time for the character and traditions of the Club to have been established.

How very different things were on the declaration of the Second World War on 3rd September 1939. The Club had by then become very well established, it had acquired a considerable reputation in the golfing world and it was financially stable, so much so that, at the Annual General Meetings in the preceding few years, the directors had been able to report comfortable surpluses – a far cry from the very early years of the Club when it was only through the generous financial concessions of its proprietor, Colonel Du Pre, that the Club was able to survive at all.

Certainly Colonel Du Pre's original aspirations to put Beaconsfield on the golfing map had been amply realised and by 1939 he must surely have been well satisfied with what had been achieved.

But then the dark clouds of war began to appear over Europe. Even as early as March 1939 Colonel Du Pre, then aged sixty-four, had raised the question at a meeting of the Committee as to what the Club should do in the event of the outbreak of war and, "after much discussion", it was unanimously agreed that the Club should be kept going for as long as possible. The secretary, Major Sutherland, was then instructed "to develop a scheme that would put that decision into effect on mobilisation".

Whether any such scheme was ever developed and committed to writing is not known, but in the early months following the declaration of war later that year the Committee found it appropriate to take various decisions and "austerity measures" that reflected the changing times. One of the first decisions was to authorise the expenditure of £14.7s.11d. on "blackout" material and then, fairly soon afterwards, decisions were made:

– to discontinue Club competitions and matches.
– to reduce the number of greenkeepers by two.

- to reduce the wages of the dressing room attendant, Mr. Hall, by 10s. a week.
- to reduce the annual staff wages allowance of £200 made to the steward "by £50 in view of the fact that the indoor staff had been reduced by one waiter".
- to allow all full and five – day members engaged in whole-time national service (whether in the Services or Home Defence) a reduced annual subscription of £2 for men and £1.11s.0d. for ladies for the duration of the war.
- to allow five-day members engaged in whole-time national service to use the Club at weekends during the war without payment of green fees.
- to consider reducing the size of the greens so as to reduce manpower requirements.
- to purchase fire fighting equipment, namely 2 buckets, 6 sandbags, 1 long-handled shovel, 1 rake and 1 stirrup pump.

Although during most of the 1930s, the directors had been able to report a comfortable surplus each year, at the first AGM after the declaration of war the directors had to report a loss of £152.16s.0d. – a loss that probably "reflected the gloom that had been spreading over the nation" during that year. Moreover, it was recognised at the same time that, for much the same reason, the Club's budget for 1939-1940 had become wholly unrealistic and so, once again, just as he had in the First World War, Colonel Du Pre came to the rescue. At a meeting of the Board in March 1940 the Colonel informed the directors that, in view of the present financial position, he would remit the rent due on 1st December 1939 and would not seek any further rent for the year ending 31st May 1940. And when, at the same meeting, it was reported that the Club's overdraft at the bank was then £533.4s.7d, Colonel Du Pre personally undertook to arrange a new overdraft limit of £1,000.

Wartime Staffing Arrangements

By March 1940 the Club secretary, Major Sutherland, had already left for military service and, initially, his wife undertook the duties of secretary. For a while, she continued to occupy the secretary's service house, Golf Lodge, on Longbottom Lane but later, not wanting to live in such a large house on her own during the war, she obtained the Club's approval to sub-let the house if a suitable tenant could be found. By October, the house had been sub-let to a Miss Laidler and Mrs. Sutherland had left. In the meantime, one of the Club's members, a Mr. P. W. Seale, had been appointed temporary secretary and he remained in that position until the end of the war.

Bob Kenyon, the professional, was released by the Club for military duties in June 1940, and there was no professional at the Club until after the war. Before Kenyon left, Colonel Du Pre had made arrangements with him as regards the stock in his shop and it was also arranged that Kenyon would take a lease of his service house, The Seventh, so that during his absence it could be sub-let to a suitable tenant. That tenant was a Mr. W. J. Wallace who took occupation in the October and remained there for the rest of the war.

Jack Cooper, the steward, enlisted in the Royal Air Force in 1940, but Mrs. Cooper continued as stewardess and, with the two maids and an additional temporary waitress at weekends, carried on the bar and catering services for some time. Mrs. Cooper remained stewardess until her husband was demobbed and returned to the Club at the end of the war.

Several of the Club's other staff were also required for military service and, so far as the course was concerned, the head greenkeeper, Ted Berry, had to make do with what, by comparison with the ten assistants that he had had previously, was but a skeleton staff. However, he did have throughout the war the benefit of the very considerable hands-on involvement of one of the members, Peter Case. Moreover, the task of maintaining the course was probably made somewhat easier when the Bucks War Agricultural Executive Committee required the Club to permit sheep to be grazed on parts of the course so that much of the land bounded by the 15th, 4th and 14th holes, which then was very open land, was fenced off for sheep grazing. Ted himself was given a 5s. a week increase in wages in 1941 as a "war bonus" for his stout efforts on the course.

Requisitions and the Threat of Invasion

As was the case with many large properties during the war including, later on, Wilton Park itself, a portion of the clubhouse was requisitioned in 1941 by H. M. Ministry of Works and Buildings and came to be occupied by the Foreign Office Wireless Section. A requisition lease was concluded and, in case any damage to the property was caused by the occupation, a Schedule of Condition was drawn up, agreed and "deposited in Mr. Langley-Taylor's strong room for safe custody".

It is not known how much of the clubhouse was requisitioned, but the Board accepted the Ministry's proposal for a rental for the occupied part at the rate of £165 per annum for the duration of the war and, thereafter, on one month's notice on either side. It was agreed that a separate claim was to be filed by the Club to recover contributions to the wages of the Club staff and other such items and so a claim in respect of 1942 was made. It included a contribution charge of 10s. per week in respect of the services of Mr. Fowler, the changing room attendant, and 3d. per week for the use of the lavatories, soap and towels. When on one occasion the Ministry wrote to the Board repudiating these additional charges the Board instructed the secretary to persist with the claim with the result that the Ministry accepted the 3d. per week charge and the Club waived the weekly charge for Fowler's services.

The following year, after a meeting with a representative of the Foreign Office, the Board agreed to the requisitioning of further parts of the clubhouse, namely the kitchen, staff room and the Top Bar at an annual rental of £50 – later increased to £55.

By 1942, Wilton Park itself had been requisitioned by the War Office to serve as one of the establishments for the highly secret activities of Combined Services Detailed Interrogation Centre (CSDIC), and Colonel and Mrs. Du Pre had vacated Wilton Park to take up residence at their house in Ascot. The White House was used as the Officers Mess, Nissen huts were erected in the grounds for the other ranks and flat-roofed brick buildings were constructed to accommodate the very high ranking German and Italian prisoners. Among the many distinguished "visitors" who spent time at Wilton Park were field Marshal von Rundstedt and Generaloberst Franz Halder and, so it is said, Rudolph Hess. It was probably as a consequence of parts of the clubhouse having been requisitioned at an earlier date that some of the club's furniture had come to be stored at Wilton Park, where it was then "let on hire to the military authorities" when the White House itself was requisitioned and used as an Officers Mess. The furniture was "derequisitioned" in 1945 and eventually returned to the Club.

The threat of invasion as early in the war as June 1940 was such that in order to discourage airborne invasion, the military authorities required steps to be taken to erect obstacles on the level fairways, "staggered barrels or concrete pylons" being suggested. It was said that an Admiral James had arranged to view the course from the air and that he would make a report. A month later it was reported to the Board that concrete pylons had been erected satisfactorily by the military authorities. Unfortunately no photographs or descriptions of these pylons exist – probably for reasons of security – but someone who, as a boy, caddied at weekends during the war, recalls that they were more like wooden pit props standing about twelve to fifteen feet tall. When Japan entered the war, a very tall mast, nicknamed "Tojo" by the locals, was erected on the highest point on the 18th fairway to "listen" to Tokyo. What with pylons and masts as "immovable obstructions" and with the scrapes of the sheep – not being "burrowing animals" – golf must have been altogether more exciting then than it is today.

The threat of invasion increased as events in Europe unfolded and in March 1941 the Club received an application from the Officer Commanding the Beaconsfield Company of the Home Guard to use the empty professional's shop as a guard room. The Board granted this request on the basis that:

- the rent would be £1 per month (payable on 1st of each month) to cover use and occupation and the supply of fuel, light and services.
- it would be for the duration of the war and thereafter terminable by one month's notice on either side.
- the Home Guard was to be responsible to make good all dilapidations.

However, it turned out not to be possible to pay rent, as such, unless the premises had been formally requisitioned, and so instead of going through that formality, it was agreed that the Club should simply submit a claim each year for fuel, light and services and if, by chance, the claim happened to come to the equivalent of £1 per month, which it did, then so be it.

In 1942 the Ministry of Works and Buildings terminated its requisition of those parts of the clubhouse occupied by the Foreign Office and the Ministry's offer of £170 plus "the partitions" (whatever they were) in settlement of the Club's claim for dilapidations was accepted. At about the same time, however, the War Department requisitioned the first floor, the top bedroom and "part of the sheds" (presumably the greenkeeping sheds) for use by the 5th Battalion of the Bucks Home Guard as offices and Quartermaster's stores. The rent was to be £185 per annum and 18s.6d. per week towards the cost of heating.

When all the premises were derequisitioned in 1946, the Southern Command's land agent made a final offer of £55 to cover all dilapidations plus £2.17s.6d. for the professional fees incurred by the Club, and this offer was accepted. The Board then engaged the building firm of Lovells, subject to their obtaining the necessary licence from the Ministry of Works, to carry out repairs and redecoration of the clubhouse – but "the sun blinds will be left till a later date".

Sadly, no photographs or descriptions of the social and golfing activities that took place at the Club during the war years have been located and probably none now exist. Obviously, given petrol shortage, food rationing, the growing shortage of golf balls and the absence of many members on war service, it was only to be expected that both golfing and social activities would be considerably reduced. This seems to be reflected in the fact that the monthly charge to the Wine Committee was reduced in 1940 by the General Committee from the budgeted £40 to £20. However, it appears that things eased a little in the following years for the charge was raised the next year to £30 per month and then to £40 in 1944. Maybe these increases merely reflected increased sales due to the presence of Ministry and military personnel. For the first year after the war ended, the Wine Committee charge was raised to £50 – with the price of whiskey and gin being raised from 1s.6d. per tot to 2s. in the case of whiskey and to 1s.9d. in the case of gin.

Life at the Club was beginning to return to normal !

And Peace Again

There are no records of any victory celebrations and competitions having been held at the Club to mark the return of peace and the home-coming of members and staff, but such an event would surely not have been allowed to pass without due recognition.

Nevertheless, somewhat surprisingly, Colonel Du Pre made no reference to any such special events when he made his presentation to the thirty-second AGM held at the clubhouse on 8th December 1945. Perhaps he was too preoccupied with the financial situation for he did have to reveal that the Club had made a loss of £376 after "a very difficult year". He went on to report that since now new members were coming in, he was hopeful that the situation would soon become normal again – especially after the clubhouse had been derequisitioned and the early return of the Club's furniture from Wilton Park was anticipated. Nevertheless, he said, it had been found necessary to increase subscriptions for those who were elected members for the first time after 1st December 1945. These would be:

	Gentlemen	*Ladies*
Full ordinary members	12 guineas	9 guineas
Members of the late Wilton Park G.C. & Five-day members	7 guineas	5 guineas
Undergraduate members	5 guineas	
Country and Non-playing members	3 guineas	
Junior members	2 guineas	

At a meeting of the directors early in 1946 Colonel Du Pre himself emphasised the need for the Club to attract young members, and his proposal that, as a temporary measure, a new Intermediate Full Membership category should be introduced for those existing and new members who were over seventeen and under twenty-six years of age was agreed. Such members were to have all the playing privileges of a full member but would only pay the five-day member's subscription.

The Staff Return

The secretary, Colonel Sutherland, was the first of the Club staff to return after the war. In fact, he had written to the Club in November 1944 regarding his return and received a reply saying that, much as they would like to see him back, the Club could not see how that could be arranged until it was known when Golf Lodge, which was still leased to Miss Laidler, would become vacant. However, as it happened, Mr. Wallace, who had taken a lease of The Seventh back in 1940, indicated in January 1945, that he would like to vacate the property and, by mutual agreement, he left at the end of May. The way was then open for Colonel Sutherland to return to the Club by occupying The Seventh on an interim basis.

In appreciation of the invaluable services that Mr. Seale had rendered to the Club as temporary secretary during the war years, the Board resolved to reinstate him as a full member at a reduced annual subscription of 4 guineas, to refund his entrance fee and to invite him to serve on the Committee.

In the absence of virtually all of the greenstaff during the war, Club records indicate that the course was kept playable almost entirely due to the considerable efforts of the head greenkeeper and one particular member, namely Peter Case, described as "a most courteous gentleman" who had been a member since the 1930s. In 1944, in recognition of his valuable services to the Club, the directors decided to refund his 1943-1944 subscription and to "give him a free subscription for the ensuing year". Several of the members wanted to show their own appreciation to Peter "for what he had done for the course during the war" and so a presentation fund was opened with a suggested upper limit of one guinea per member. The fund eventually came to just under £60 and the presentation was made to him in the clubhouse at lunch-time on 6th October. The same year, Peter was elected a director and played a significant role in the formation of the members' Club a few years later. When he died in 1975 aged ninety-three, Peter had been retired for no less than thirty-seven years.

In July 1945, Bob Kenyon wrote to the Club asking what terms the directors were prepared to offer him if he returned to his position as professional on his release from the services. When the Club indicated that they would welcome him back on the same terms as had been applicable when he left, he tendered his resignation and took up a position at the Worsley Golf Club in Manchester.

Some six professionals applied for the vacancy when it was advertised and Jimmy Adams, who immediately before the war had been the professional at Royal Liverpool Golf Club, emerged as the favoured candidate. After being interviewed by Colonel Du Pre at the Club, he was duly appointed professional in January 1946. Having been born in Troon in 1910, Jimmy had turned professional when he was fourteen and had become one of the top names in British professional golf by the time of his appointment. He had been runner-up in the Open in 1926 and 1938, had won the Penfold Tournament in 1936 and was named as one of the eight members of the 1939 Ryder Cup team. That match was, of course, not played because of the outbreak of war.

When Jack Cooper, the steward, returned from the war in mid-1945, the interim agreement with Mrs. Cooper was terminated and new terms for their joint employment were agreed. They were to receive £250 salary plus a bonus of £50 and a transport allowance of £25 – this latter to cover the cost of travelling to and from the Club to purchase groceries for the Club. As before, the kitchen staff were to be engaged by the steward but paid by the Club up to a total limit of £200 per annum. The steward was to remain fully responsible for catering and to continue to be entitled to eighty percent of any profit and to bear twenty percent of any loss.

The war was over. The members were returning. There was a full complement of staff. And all seemed well with the world. But, sadly, it was not to last.

The Passing of a Friend and the End of an Era

The euphoria that followed the ending of the war was very soon cut short so far as Beaconsfield Golf Club was concerned for on 23rd August 1946 Colonel Du Pre, then aged seventy-one, died at his home, Tetworth, in Ascot. The cause of death is not known, but he does not appear to have been ill for long because he attended meetings of the Board and the Committee as late as May that year.

It fell to Sir Alexander Murray, who had been captain of the Club from 1936 to 1939 and who had been elected to the Board in 1938, to chair the meeting of the directors on 21st September 1946 at which the news of the chairman's death was formally noted. Leonard Padfield and Peter Case, who had been elected directors in 1944 and 1946 respectively, were the other two directors present at that meeting. After Sir Alexander had been elected chairman of the Board, it was agreed to record the following resolution in the minutes and to send a copy to the Colonel's widow. The resolution read:

> The Directors and Members of the Committee of Beaconsfield Golf Club desire to place on record their very sincere regret at the death of Colonel Du Pre, and to express to Mrs. Du Pre and his family their deepest sympathy with them in their very sad bereavement.
>
> The Directors and Committee feel very strongly that the Club owes its existence solely to the inspiration of Colonel Du Pre, without whose active and generous support it would not have been carried on since its inception over thirty years ago, and that it has undoubtedly added to the amenities of the whole neighbourhood.
>
> The Members of the Club desire to be associated in this expression of their very real regret and sympathy at the passing of a friend.

Colonel Du Pre was cremated following a private family funeral, but memorial services were later held at the Parish Church of St Mary and All Saints in Beaconsfield and at the parish church in Ascot. Among the many people from the Club who attended the memorial service at Beaconsfield were the secretary, Colonel Sutherland and Mrs. Sutherland, Sir Alexander Murray and the other directors, Mrs. Bunty Duncan, representing the Ladies' section, Mr. and Mrs. Langley-Taylor, Mr. Jack Cooper, the steward, representing the Artisans Golfing Society, Mr. Jimmy Adams, the professional, and Mr. Ted Berry, the head greenkeeper.

Lt. Colonel Fleetwood Pellew, who had been the first secretary of the Club in 1914 and who was a nephew of Colonel Du Pre, was also present. He, Francis James Du Pre and Langley-Taylor were the executors of Colonel Du Pre's will and they were soon to play a very significant role in the Club's future.

IN MEMORY OF
LT-COL. WILLIAM BARING DU PRE. DL. JP.
OF WILTON PARK. BEACONSFIELD
WHO DIED ON 23rd AUGUST 1946 AGED 71
AND OF HIS WIFE
YOURI WYNYARD DU PRE
WHO DIED ON 19th MAY 1942 AGED 62
THIS TABLET WAS ERECTED BY THEIR DAUGHTERS

The wall tablet memorial in Beaconsfield Parish Church

At the meeting of the directors on 21st September 1946 at which the news of Colonel Du Pre's death had been formally noted, it was agreed to invite Langley-Taylor to become a director of the company "subject to the agreement of Colonel Du Pre's executors". Langley-Taylor accepted the invitation and was set to become the invaluable link in the coming years between the Club and the Du Pre estate.

Following the death of Colonel Du Pre and the resignation of Mr. Seale due to ill health, there were two vacancies on the Committee and, at their meeting in November 1946, the directors invited Mr. Andrew Wylie, who had been a member since 1934, to fill one of those vacancies and he accepted. Andrew was to play a major role in the establishment and development of the Club in the coming years.

Even without the death of its founder and proprietor, life for the Club in the immediate post-war period was always going to be difficult, and this was highlighted by Sir Alexander Murray at the thirty-third AGM which had been postponed to January 1947 because of Colonel Du Pre's death. Sir Alexander, reporting on the audited accounts, acknowledged that there had been an increase in annual subscription income of £603 over the previous year, bringing the total subscription income of £2,156 to the highest it had been for five years. However, the return of the secretary, the steward and the professional from war service had added considerably to expenditure on salaries and wages and the derequisitioning of the clubhouse had meant that

LIST OF OFFICERS
OF THE
Beaconsfield Golf Club.
1947.

President:
VISCOUNT CURSON

Captain:
C. RISSIK

COMMITTEE:
SIR ALEXANDER R. MURRAY, K.C.I.E., C.B.E.
L. PADFIELD, M.C.
G. LANGLEY-TAYLOR   A. P. CASE
H. B. HOLME   W. L. ROBERTSON   A. R. WYLIE

Secretary:
LT.-COL. H. O. SUTHERLAND

LADIES:

President:
MRS. HERBERT

1st Team Captain   *2nd Team Captain*
MRS. K. V. BRADDON   MRS. OWEN DAVIES

COMMITTEE:
MRS. L. PADFIELD   MRS. ALEC GOLD   MRS. H. O. SUTHERLAND
MISS BARNETT   MISS MACFARLANE

Hon. Secretary:
MRS. F. J. DUNCAN

Telephone : Beaconsfield 1260

The officers of the club in 1947

there had also been a reduction in rental income. These items, taken with increases in salaries and wages generally, had resulted in the Club making a loss of £705 compared with the loss of £376 the previous year. Sir Alexander emphasised that, while proper economy would continue to be exercised, increased expenditure on the upkeep and maintenance of the clubhouse and the course would have to be faced and every effort would have to be made to attract new members.

Thus a long and successful chapter in the history of Beaconsfield Golf Club had come to an end and, for the very first time since it was founded in 1914, the Club's List of Officers published in 1947 appeared without the name of Colonel William Baring Du Pre.

It was time for a new era to begin.

Chapter Nine

The Dawn of the New Era
1946 to 1948

Golf and Social Activities Return

O NCE THE staff and the members had returned from their wartime activities, life at the Club fairly soon returned to something approaching normality even though food rationing and petrol shortages continued.

Competitions and medals were soon resumed and records show the following successes in the named trophy events played in the two years immediately following the war:

	1946	1947
Club Championship	W. L. Robertson	K. V. Braddon
Beaconsfield Challenge Bowl	A. P. Case	W. L. Robertson
The Grange Cup	J. I. Bracey-Gibbon	H. L. Whitworth-Jones
Sir John Aird Cup	J. I. Bracey-Gibbon	W. L. Robertson
The Lewis Pawle Trophy	W. L. Robertson	A. R. Wylie
The Montrose Cloete Cup	F. W. K. Duncan	H. L. Whitworth-Jones

The Lewis Pawle Trophy which had been won in 1938 by Gordon Le Mare, the father of Robert Le Mare who is still a member, was mislaid during the war years and the £10 insurance money was used to purchase a new trophy which is the one actually played for today.

By 1947, inter-club matches had been resumed and in June the Club beat Denham away by 9 matches to 3 and Berkhamsted away by 7 matches to 5. At the same time, golfing societies began to reappear at Beaconsfield with the Hazards Golfing Society and the Buyers Benevolent Association being among the first.

Unfortunately, the younger lady members' eagerness to play was, as always, tempered by the demands of motherhood and this led one of the Committee members, Mr. Holmes, to suggest that the Club run a crèche to enable them to play more golf. Having sympathy with the idea, the Committee instructed the secretary to ascertain if the W.V.S. would be likely to help. He later reported that he had spoken to one of the lady members, Nancye Gold, and discovered that a Mrs. Diamond was in charge of the W.V.S. in the district, but that Mrs. Gold did not think that the W.V.S. would take to the idea. As it turned out, she was right and so the well-meaning proposal was dropped.

Social events began to be organised again. Towards the end of 1946, a Dance Committee was formed under the chairmanship of Peter Case, and this resulted in a very successful dance being held on 31st January – and making a welcome profit of £84.14s.2d. for Club funds. Not surprisingly, the Board asked Peter Case to organise another dance for mid-summer.

Bridge was also resumed its place in the Club's activities, so much so that the directors soon found it necessary to establish certain "House Rules" for bridge played at the Club. These were that:

- not more than two players may "cut in" at a table.
- not more than four may play two consecutive rubbers if other members are waiting to "cut in".
- "club points" may not exceed 3d. per hundred.
- "table money" to be 1s. per player for the cards.

And, in so far as bar consumption can be regarded a measure of the social success of a Club, it must have been pleasing to record that the Club's charge to the Wine Committee for 1946 was increased from the previous year's £600 to £1,000.

A New Lease and a New Company

Even before the death of Colonel Du Pre, the question of the renewal of the Club's lease had arisen. The Colonel himself was, of course, in a somewhat unusual situation for, as the life tenant of the Wilton Park estate, he was the lessor, and, as chairman of Beaconsfield Golf Club Ltd., he also represented the lessee. Nevertheless, he obviously conducted the discussions about the renewal of the lease with an even-handedness that impressed the directors such that, at their meeting in November 1944, they recorded their "warm appreciation" for the way in which he had responded to their suggested amendments to the proposed renewal terms.

There seems to have been no undue haste on either party's side to finalise the renewal and the matter dragged on for many months; it was probably only the Colonel's death in August 1946 that brought some urgency to the matter. At their meeting the following December, the directors reviewed the draft lease and related tenancy agreements that had been approved by the Colonel before his death. The renewed lease of the course, the clubhouse, the two semi-detached houses on Farm Lane and the houses known as The

Seventh and Golf Lodge[†] was to be for a period of seven years from 29th September 1946, but it could be terminated by either party after four years. The related tenancy agreements covered five pieces of land on the periphery of the course that had been within the original lease but had been separated out because they were only going to be leased to the Club for a period of one year certain and thereafter terminable on three months' notice. One of the amendments that the Club managed to obtain was that the rights of "guests at and occupiers of Wilton Park to play on the course free of charge" was restricted to members of the Du Pre family. Subject to the various amendments, the directors agreed to the proposed lease and tenancy agreements and the formalities were completed on 3rd April 1947.

However, in a letter to the Club later that same year, Colonel Du Pre's executors indicated that the Du Pre family did not wish to continue to be involved with the golf Club and that therefore they, the executors, were prepared to consider selling the shares, debentures and other assets and goodwill of Beaconsfield Golf Club Ltd. to the Club's members if they were interested. The members were, indeed, interested and, at a meeting of the members on 24th May 1947, they authorised two of their number, Sir Alexander Murray and Leonard Padfield, to negotiate with the executors on their behalf. In order to facilitate the asset transfer process, a new members' company limited by guarantee in the amount of £1 per member was incorporated on 13th May 1948 and, since it was not possible to have two companies registered with the same name, the new company was temporarily and most aptly given the name of the Wilton Park Golf Club Ltd.

Negotiations with the executors over the next few months covered not only the value of the furniture, fittings, equipment and other assets of the old company, but also the terms of a longer lease that would be required for the protection of the interests of the new members' company. Ultimately agreement was reached for the recently renewed lease to be surrendered and to be replaced by a twenty-one year lease of the same properties (with the exception of Golf Lodge) at a rent of £600 per annum, and for the sale and purchase of the Club's total assets at a net price of £3,532. The formalities of these transactions were completed in July 1948.

The following month the first General Meeting of the new company, still called Wilton Park Golf Club, was held at the clubhouse primarily for the purpose of electing officers and directors. But in opening the meeting, Sir Alexander Murray was at pains to emphasise the difficult financial situation that the Club faced. He drew attention to the onerous full repairing covenants in the lease and to the fact that few repairs had been carried out by the late lessees. He also drew attention to the obligations

---

†Golf Lodge later became known as Kilcool and is now known as Bradgate.

to maintain the driveway and many fences and said that all these obligations would require substantial reserves to be built up. Sir Alexander reported that, as at the date of that meeting, 184 men and 80 ladies had applied for membership of the new members' club, but he felt that at least 30 more men and 30 more ladies paying full playing subscriptions would be needed if the Club's current working loss were to be turned into a surplus. Debentures, he said, were another means of supporting the Club and were available in units of £5 each up to a limit of £250 per member. Already there were 155 debenture holders and he encouraged other members to apply. In fact, to ease these financial difficulties the Board decided in 1949 to issue £8,000 of non-interest-bearing debentures (the "1949 Debentures'). These were undated with repayment at par and with only the Club having the right of redemption. The bank was appointed as trustee with the assets of the Club pledged as security.

The purchase of these debentures by the then members of the Club was in effect a generous gesture of support by the subscribers, for amounts of £100 and £200 were significant at a time when a salary of £1,000 a year was a substantial one. For the Club, the debentures were a key element in its financial viability. However, inflation over the years seriously reduced the value of the debentures for the holders and, although the Club had a policy later of repaying debentures on request, often on the death of the holder, inflation also reduced their significance in its liabilities as the Club's income and financial stability improved.

In 1994 it was decided to attempt to repay all the remaining debentures, then amounting to £3,470 as at 31st May, but only the holders of some £790 worth could be traced and paid. It was then agreed with the trustee that three members of the Club would be appointed trustees and this finally released the charge on the Club's assets. Any remaining debentures that come to light will, of course, be paid off.

At the elections held at the first General Meeting of the new members' Club in August 1948, the following were voted into office:

President   Sir Alexander Murray

Captain   Andrew Wylie

Directors   W. T. Birch, Ken Braddon, Peter Case, Florence Duncan, A. H. Gold, E. B. Irwin, Leonard Padfield, Vesey Raffety, Lindsay Robertson.

And so the distinction and, indeed, challenge of becoming the first captain of the new members' Club fell to Andrew Wylie. Andrew had become a member of the Club in 1934 after his return from business overseas and, in the coming years, he was to play a significant role in guiding the new company through its financial difficulties and in developing a wider scope of membership for the Club.

As had been agreed, on the voluntary winding up of the original company, its name was transferred to the new members company which was registered on 28th July 1949 as the new "Beaconsfield Golf Club Limited".

Most of what remained of the Wilton Park estate was sold by the Du Pre trustees to the Ministry of Defence in 1959 and the White House itself was demolished in 1967 and replaced by the highly visible tower block complex.

The old order had changed and had yielded place to the new. The proprietary Club had given place to the members' Club – and a new era had begun.

*The tower block complex with the White House in the centre
about to be demolished*

Chapter Ten

The Members' Club
1948 to 2002

The Freehold Purchase

SCARCELY HAD the new members' Club settled down after the initial changes that followed the death of Colonel Du Pre than events took yet another and unexpected turn – a turn that was to put considerable stress on the management and the members of the new Club for several years.

In May 1950, the Board received a letter from George Langley-Taylor, acting on behalf of the executors of Colonel Du Pre's estate, indicating that, if the members were interested, the executors would be prepared to sell the freehold of the leased property to the Club for £25,000. Most of the members, though by no means all of them, were indeed interested but not at the price that had been proposed. There followed several months of negotiations with the executors, with the Club placing considerable emphasis in its bargaining on the extensive repairs that a recent survey had shown to be necessary, not only to the clubhouse itself, but also to another of the leased properties, Golf Cottage (formerly known as The Seventh). The need for these repairs, it was emphasised, was the result of neglect by the former lessees (i.e. the original Beaconsfield Golf Club) and had to be reflected in the price. The members' initial offer of £10,000 was rejected by the executors and so a members' meeting was called in June 1951 to approve a revised offer by the Club. With the approval of the majority of the members present and voting and with the consent of the 1949 debenture holders, a revised offer of £12,000 was made and eventually accepted by the executors. Mr. Whitley-Jones, who had been a member of the Club since 1934 and who became president in 1958, arranged a Building Society loan for the Club of £12,000 at four percent repayable over twenty years and completion took place on 22nd November 1951. The lessee had become the freehold owner.

The executors had also agreed that the Club should have a ten year option to purchase for £200 some 3.6 acres of land abutting Longbottom Lane to the east of Golf Lodge. This option was included in the conveyance and, in accordance with its continuing policy regarding neighbouring land, the Club exercised that option in 1961.

Financial Difficulties

And so it was that the new Club could face the future as the freehold owner of its own clubhouse and its own course – but it was a future that was to be beset with financial difficulties for many years. Although the Club's negotiators had been extremely successful in securing the freehold for a very reasonable price, the points that they had made in their negotiations about the state of repair of the properties were not fanciful and had to be addressed. In addition, new equipment for the course was needed to improve its condition and staff wages continued to rise. There were serious financial difficulties from the very beginning and, without the commitment to the Club of those members who purchased the debentures, it is doubtful if the Club could have survived.

Many and varied ways of increasing income to make ends meet were tried. Members were continually exhorted to encourage golfing societies with whom they were associated to arrange weekday fixtures at Beaconsfield. A football syndicate for members, set up by Lt. Colonel Taylor when he was on the Board, was run for several years, even while he was captain. Unfortunately, although the syndicate won £9.7s. on its first entry, at the end of the first year it only managed to hand over £12.10s. to Club funds and it never managed to make a significant contribution.

A much more productive source of income was the Club raffles, although one of them held in 1950 led to a somewhat embarrassing situation when, at the instigation of the Post Office, the president and two other directors of the Club were interviewed by the Divisional Inspector of Buckinghamshire Constabulary at the clubhouse in connection with an investigation into a possible infringement of the betting and gaming law. Happily, after giving the Club "a serious caution as to future conduct", the police decided to take no further action – and the Club's funds benefited from the raffle by a very welcome £407.

Some measure of the continuing financial difficulties with which the Club was faced can found in the report of the Finance Committee to the Board in 1955:

> The cash position will become serious by the end of the current year. Every year the cash is depleted by the capital repayment to the Building Society and for the current year the sum involved is approximately £430. In addition, we have invested £270 in new gang mowers and a rotary mower and so we have had to find over £700 for capital items. If, as seems likely, the surplus for the current year is very much the same as in 1954-1955 at say £200, we shall find the cash position worse by £500 at the end of the financial year and that would mean a bank overdraft. In subsequent years, the position would become progressively worse and

Harold Staines (captain), "Gunga" Dean (secretary), Bunty Duncan (ladies captain),
Leonard Padfield (president) and Peter Case (immediate past captain) in 1958

the time is rapidly approaching when we will be faced with either raising more capital in some form or other or finding ways and means of increasing the annual surplus so as to cover our capital commitments.

Despite this recognition of the problems, the financial position continued to deteriorate mainly due to a significant fall in membership and to increasing staff costs. When, two years later, income was more than £900 below budget, the Board set up a select committee "to review all possible ways of reducing costs and increasing income". The committee was chaired by the captain, Harold Staines, with Whitley-Jones, Lindsay Robertson, Vesey Raffety and Andrew Wylie (co-opted) as the other members. In addition to accepting the committee's recommendations to increase the price of green fees, spirits and wines and to increase the artisans' subscriptions from £3 to £4, the Board also accepted the committee's principal recommendation to bite the bullet and progressively increase subscriptions. As anticipated, when that policy was implemented it did produce a few immediate resignations, but it significantly increased the Club's income over the next few years and, equally importantly, it did not have the negative effect of deterring new applications for membership that some had feared; during the next three years membership increased from 457 to 511.

It was only through the tireless efforts and commitment of the Board and the members during those pioneering years that the Club eventually

Val Doonican

emerged in the 1970s from its financial difficulties. And if individuals had to be named for their particular efforts on behalf of the Club, they would unquestionably include Andrew Wylie, the first captain of the members' Club, and Harold Staines, who was elected captain in 1957, president from 1975 to 1979 and was made a life member in 1983.

And since those difficult days, the members' Club has continued to prosper and to maintain its objective of being a traditional members' Club. Rather than looking like extracts from *Burke's Peerage* and the military *Lists*, its membership list became much more representative of the professions, of industry and of commerce and this was deliberate policy from the time of its first captain, Andrew Wylie, onwards. That is not to say that the Club has not had its fair share of celebrities from different walks of life; Dennis Compton, Stanley Holloway, Joan Hammond and Nancy Mitchell were some of the celebrities who were members in the 1950s and 1960s, and there are still celebrity members today but it would be much too indelicate of the author to categorise fellow members in that way. Because of his sketches for the book, mention of Val Doonican may perhaps be made as one of the current celebrities.

Social activities have never assumed a dominant role at Beaconsfield, but the traditional formal events of a golf club such as the New Year's Eve Dinner Dance and the Summer Ball have continued to be held with only few breaks ever since they were started way back in Colonel Du Pre's time. A variety of informal supper evenings and other entertainment are arranged for the winter months by hard working Social Committees, but most of the informal social occasions take place in connection with golfing events such as the Turkey Foursomes, Around ye Houses on Boxing Day morning, and the mixed foursomes events. Bridge still occupies a significant place in the social calendar. From time to time there have been suggestions that the Club should have tennis courts and a swimming pool and perhaps even become a Golf and Country Club, but these have never found majority support.

When Burns Night was first celebrated at the Club in 1984, it was a stag night in the Men's Bar and, so it is recorded (probably by a Sassenach), "the attendance was dismal". Since then, it has become one of the Club's most

Keith Wilcox, secretary, and his administrative staff – Summer 2002
Left to right: Dianne Regan, Catherine Daymond-John and Liz Smythson

popular social events open to both men and women and its continued popularity was not even diminished when, in proposing "The Immortal Memory" on a recent occasion, Andrew Tait took it upon himself to seek to prove that Burns was a more celebrated writer than Shakespeare.

The efficiency of a golf club depends to a very large extent on its secretary as does its whole social atmosphere. In this regard, Beaconsfield has for the most part been very fortunate in its appointments, and to its several secretaries[†] must go much of the credit for its continued success. For the fifty years following the first incorporation of the Club in 1914, every secretary had

†See Appendix 1.

Ivor Anderson, secretary from 1988 to 1996

Jack Cooper, steward from 1938 to 1948, playing for the Golf Club Stewards Association in their match against the Golf Club Secretaries Association at Beaconsfield, 1947

been a retired army officer – invariably a Lt. Colonel – but with the appointment of Charles Crockwell in 1964 the mould was broken. Charles, who had been a member for many years and captain in 1961, took on the role of secretary from 1964 to 1969. John Anderson and Jimmy Adair were other members of the Club who also acted as secretary for short periods as did Ken Kingshott who took on the responsibilities of secretary, albeit for only four months, when in 1986, the person who had been appointed to become secretary suddenly died the day before he was due to take up his duties.

The two longest serving secretaries in recent times have been Michael Hunter, who had previously been secretary at Moor Park, and Ivor Anderson, who had been at Berkhamsted. Both of them were professional in their handling of the ever increasing scope and complexity of a secretary's responsibilities and were extremely popular with the membership – something not given to all secretaries. The occasions of their leaving, Michael for another position and Ivor for retirement, reflected the warmth and affection in which they were held. The present secretary, Keith Wilcox, was appointed in 2001 having previously been at Formby.

The Stewardship

As if the difficult financial situation facing the new members' Club in 1948 and the departure of Jimmy Adams, the professional, were not enough, the Board soon had another problem to face.

Jack Cooper, had returned from military service at the end of the war to resume his position as steward of the Club with his wife as stewardess. Jack had always been a great supporter of and participant in the activities of the Golf Stewards Association and as its Chairman in 1947, he was able to arrange for the first post-war annual match against the Golf Club Secretaries Association to be played at Beaconsfield that July. Tom Scott, the editor, began his account of the match in *Golf Illustrated* with the words:

Lt. Colonel Sutherland, secretary, playing for the Golf Club Secretaries in the same match

Take one picturesque golf course, add a friendly, hospitable clubhouse, then take a number of keen golfers enjoying every minute of the day. Mix well together and you have the match between the Golf Secretaries Association and the Golf Stewards Association at Beaconsfield.

Although Jack's own enjoyment of the match was probably marred by his team's defeat by 8 matches to 4, it was obviously a very successful day that was enjoyed as much as anyone by Beaconsfield's own secretary, Lt. Colonel Sutherland, complete with his "portable caddie". The annual match between the two Associations returned to Beaconsfield several times after that.

Jack and his wife were very popular figures at the Club and Jack was also very much involved with the activities of the Artisan's Club of which, except for the war years, he was honorary secretary and treasurer from 1938 until 1949. It was therefore a relatively easy matter for the Board of the new members' Club to decide to retain him and his wife as steward and stewardess. However, the Coopers were unable to accept the new terms of employment that the Board offered them in August 1948 and, after several discussions over the following weeks, the Coopers eventually tendered their resignation – very much at the same time as Jimmy Adams tendered his. *Golf Illustrated* duly reported these events:

Beaconsfield Golf Club faces a double departure from their staff. As well as Jimmy Adams going to Wentworth, their capable and popular steward, Jack Cooper, is leaving. Jack is changing his vocations, but only slightly – he is to become a Boniface. We can imagine no one more in character as "mein host".

Rick Bell, steward from 1986 to 2000, and his wife Barbara

In fact, the Coopers left to become licencees of The Crispin public house in Burnham. Jack later joined Burnham Beeches Golf Club and remained a member there until his death in 1987, but he returned to play at Beaconsfield on several occasions, including the 1974 Autumn Meeting of the Golf Club Stewards Association. Jack's second wife, Joyce, was Ladies' captain at Burnham Beeches in 2000 – but she still fondly recalls buying her very first set of clubs from Alex Crombie at Beaconsfield.

Since the Coopers, the longest serving steward has been Rick Bell who, with his wife, Barbara, came to the Club in January 1986. Competent as he undoubtedly was in dealing with the many and varied tasks of a club steward, it was as Toastmaster and Master of Ceremonies that Rick brought that extra dimension to club functions, to weddings and to other events at the Club. His stature, his demeanour, his remarkable ability to remember names and his uncanny ability to judge precisely the line to be drawn between members and staff marked him out as a very special person who will long be remembered by members and visitors alike. In his earlier years, when he was in the Scots Guards and the Metropolitan Police, Rick had been a keen sportsman but, in more recent times, an investment interest in steeple-chasing became his principal "sport" – apart, that is, from his appearance in the annual match between the Club and the Staff and Board. His pairing in those matches with Christine Watson when she was a member of the Board was certainly the height of his golfing career – though perhaps not of hers. On the occasion of Rick and Barbara's retirement evening in November 2000, the clubhouse was overwhelmed with members coming to express their appreciation and to wish them well; no-one could remember any occasion when so many members had gathered at the Club and the warmth and humour of Rick's farewell speech will long be remembered.

The unenviable task of following such a personality has fallen on the shoulders of David Jennings who took up the new position of clubhouse manager in December 2000. David is his own man with his own style and measures up well to the responsibilities of this new post.

Catering and bar staff, Summer 2002

Left to right: Jose Edwards, Pauline Hore, Keith Graham, David Jennings (house manager), Rory Askew, Lauren Fabia and Maria Rodriguez Herrero.

Left to right: Alf Jones, Ann Batchelor and Pauline Hore (bar staff), Richard Batchelor (locker room attendant) with David Jennings (house manager in the centre)

The Sundowners

It would be wholly inappropriate to leave the subject of the stewardship of the Club without mention of a group of members who have for long been associated with the stewardship of the bar – a group of members who make it their custom after work to call at the clubhouse for a drink, or perhaps two, with friends while they put the world to right, before going home to dinner. The Sundowners, as they are known, are by their very nature an undefined and fluctuating group of members, but fortunately there has always been a nucleus of regulars to ensure the continuance of the custom – but even they have to admit that it is "not quite like the good old days" – a reference it seems to the days when Bob Hornall was still alive. Though regular playing members of the Club, the Sundowners do emerge as such once or twice a year for an eighteen hole competition among themselves followed by a meal – and no doubt a visit to the bar. Their generosity to the Club is not limited to their contribution to bar profits but has extended, for example, to making a donation of £60 towards the replacement of trees lost in the hurricane of October 1987 and to donating the sundial in the flower bed on the east side of the clubhouse. Long may the sun shine on the Sundowners.

Clubhouse Modifications

The financial situation of the new members' Club precluded any serious thought being given to any major changes to the clubhouse for several years, but as that situation changed various ideas to "improve" the clubhouse emerged.

There was, for example, the so-called "Whaley Plan" in 1968, named after the former captain who proposed it, which was to move the bar and lounge upstairs, to bring the dining room downstairs and to build a new staircase directly from the Men's changing room to the upstairs lounge. That proposal lay on the table for several years until it was virtually laid to rest (though perhaps not actually interred) in 1977 mainly on the grounds of its cost which at that time was estimated to be about £45,000.

There was also a proposal to extend the lounge by enclosing the verandah with glass sliding doors and to have a walled patio outside it. There had already been a flat roof extension to the original secretary's office (now the Members' Room) in 1971† but there were subsequent proposals to move that office away from that area altogether.

The Whaley Plan was one of a package of various proposals that was put to the members at a General Meeting in 1977 and, while no decisions were asked of the meeting, disparate views were passionately expressed. From that

†At the same time, a flat roof extension was made to the Ladies Dressing Room in order to provide more space and to preserve the external symmetry of the building.

The members bar, 1970

experience, the Board concluded that, while the membership would seem to go together with several of the proposals, there was strong opposition to any radical alterations to the Men's Bar, to any move of the secretary's office and to the construction of a walled patio.

The Bar and the "Imperatif"

One of the first matters discussed by the Board after it became a members' Club was the need to extend the bar into the lounge, for at that time the only means of getting drinks in the lounge directly from the bar was through a small hatchway. As early as 1949, permission had been obtained from Langley-Taylor, representing the lessors, to make the appropriate structural alterations, but before any progress had been made, the Board decided that lady members would be allowed to use the Men's Bar after 4 p.m. on Saturdays and Sundays and that therefore "the idea of a bar extension should be held in abeyance". Nevertheless, it was obvious that that did not address the real problem and, at its very next meeting, the Board adopted an entirely different solution. This was to have a "portable bar" set up in the lounge on Sundays between 12 noon and 1 p.m. for which an additional waiter would be engaged at 4s.6d. an hour. No doubt a waiter was initially engaged to service it, but it was not long before members themselves were taking turns to staff the portable bar where it was said to be imperative for members to have an aperatif before lunch. That was the origin of the Sunday morning bar that was to become known for several years as the "Imperatif" bar and the wrought iron "Imperatif" sign still hangs in the north bay window of the lounge as a reminder of this part of the Club's history. By the mid-1970s, however, the Imperatif bar had been discontinued, partly because draught beer was not available there and partly because it had become so little used. An attempt in the 1980s to revive the institution was not successful.

The Men's Bar itself had been enlarged and modernised in 1963-1964, but the need to provide better staff and beer cooling facilities behind the bar, and also to extend the bar into the lounge, remained. When these works were eventually carried out the cost of constructing extensions with pitched roofs in keeping with the rest of the building was found to be wholly disproportionate – hence the extensions have flat roofs. Unfortunately, the latter of these extensions necessitated a new external wall being built in such a position that it encroached into the front porch of the clubhouse and conceals part of the inscription "Beaconsfield Golf Club Ltd" which was carved on the outward face of the beam over the front porch when the clubhouse was built.

As this book goes to print, the Board is finalising further proposals to upgrade and refurbish what is now designated the Members' Bar.

The Secretary's Office

Despite the 1971 extension to the secretary's office, it was not long before that proved to be inadequate and so, notwithstanding the views that had been expressed at the 1977 General Meeting and the protests from the Ladies' section who had used the room proposed to be the new secretary's office "for the occasional playing of Bridge", the office was moved upstairs in 1982. The former office became the Members' Room where some of the Club's memorabilia are now displayed. Three years later, the secretary's own office was moved to the room overlooking the 18th green where it has since remained and the office that he had previously occupied became, as it is now, the general office.

The Men's Locker Room

Of the more recent alterations to the clubhouse, the most significant has undoubtedly been the enlargement and complete refurbishment of the men's locker room area together with the enlargement of the professional's shop. Of the various proposals for this modification developed by the architect, Jim Bell, the one chosen was the one specifically designed to maintain the original character of the locker room. It was by far the most extensive and expensive modification undertaken by the Club, but considerable prior consultation ensured membership support for what was a very costly, but much needed, modification.

Subsequently, although not enlarged, the Ladies Dressing Room was also substantially refurbished.

A Casualty Clearing Station

The clubhouse underwent an unusual modification, not of its structure but of its use, on Friday 11th December 1981. That was the day it came to be used more as a casualty clearing station than a clubhouse for at the height of the rush hour that morning, there was a train crash in the 150ft deep cutting near the railway bridge on Potkiln Lane. Deep snow lay on the ground at the time and there were blizzard conditions which, together with the depth of the cutting, created such extreme difficulties for the rescue services that the injured and passengers were taken along the track to the clubhouse where shelter and hot refreshments were available and where the telephones could be used free of charge. Following the incident, the Club received a huge number of letters of appreciation from those involved in the crash as well as from London Transport and Thames Valley Police.

The front porch and door by Val Doonican

Chapter Eleven

The Members' Club
1948 to 2002 – The Golfing Scene

The Beaconsfield Professionals

Jimmy Adams

WHEN BOB KENYON did not rejoin the Club as professional after the war, Jimmy Adams was appointed in his place as from January 1946 Jimmy was already a very successful golfer who had won several professional tournaments before the war and had been selected for the 1939 Ryder Cup Team.† It therefore came as no surprise when, in August 1947, the Club received a letter from the PGA asking if leave of absence could be given to Adams to play in the Ryder Cup match at Portland, Oregon, later that year. The Club readily granted leave but, by the time Adams returned from America, the Board was already considering the formation of the new members' Club and which of the existing staff it would want to retain.

Jimmy's agreement with the Club entitled him to rent free occupation of The Seventh, but under the renewal lease that had been proposed to the members' Club, the secretary's house, Golf Lodge, was excluded and would no longer be available for Club staff. In this situation, the Board decided that the secretary should move into The Seventh and that alternative arrangements would have to be made for the professional. Consequently, the offer to re-engage Adams as professional with the new members' Club was on the basis that he would have rent free occupation of The Seventh until 25th May 1948, and then, if at that time no other good accommodation was available for him, he would have to make his own arrangements and the Club would make him a housing allowance of an amount to be mutually agreed. However, after several discussions with the Club during 1948 about accommodation and about his absences to play in competitions for more than the permitted sixty-five "playing days" a year, Adams tendered his resignation in October and left at the end of

†In the event, this match was not played because of the outbreak of war.

1948 to take up the professional's post at Wentworth in succession to Archie Compston.

It had always been an important part of Colonel Du Pre's strategy for making Beaconsfield one of the leading clubs in the London area to engage a leading tournament player as the club's professional. Percy Alliss, Bob Kenyon and Jimmy Adams had all been in this mould. But the departure of Jimmy Adams gave the new members' Club the opportunity to review that policy in the light of its own members' needs and of the much higher costs that had come to be involved in engaging an established tournament player. As at many clubs after the war, the Board decided that what the Club needed was a first class,

Jimmy Adams – professional at Beaconsfield from 1946 to 1948

traditional club professional rather than a frequently absent tournament player. It is a remarkable fact that since the time of that decision over half a century ago, there have only been two professionals at Beaconsfield – namely Alex Crombie and Mike Brothers.

Alex Crombie

Alex took up his duties in succession to Jimmy Adams just before Christmas 1948. He had joined the PGA in 1938 when he was at Radlett Golf Club and came to Beaconsfield from the Golf Club Grand – Ducal de Luxembourg.

Alex fitted extremely well into the new scene at Beaconsfield and was soon recognised as a very competent teacher as well as a sympathetic listener to members' tales of woe and tragedy out on the course. Writing to the Club forty years later, an American attorney now living in Denver, Colorado, whose family had lived in Chalfont St Giles for several years after the war, said: "At ten shillings a half hour lesson from Mr. Crombie was an investment of a lifetime. He was a wonderful teacher." There are several members of the Club today who would readily agree. And being a natural teacher, he was very much involved in the early golf lessons for juniors that were organised mainly by the Ladies' section.

111

Alex Crombie, professional at Beaconsfield from 1948 to 1973

Having been at the Club for ten years, Alex was made an Honorary Member in January 1959, and when two years later he married, the Club gave him a cheque for £30 as a wedding present and the members contributed to a separate present.

During his time at Beaconsfield, Alex had several assistants, one of whom was Jimmy Hume, who came from Gullane, went on to become the professional at Harewood Downs and is now back as professional at Gullane.

When in 1971, Alex became ill, Frank Randall, a member of the Artisans' Club, was able to look after the shop in his absence and the Club made payments to Alex to offset the substantial loss of his income from teaching. Sadly, Alex never fully recovered from the illness and died in 1973 after a quarter of a century with the Club.

Mike Brothers

Having developed an interest in golf as a boy caddie at Denham, it was probably no surprise that when he left school Mike Brothers became an assistant to John Sheridan, Denham's very long-serving professional. It was while he was with John that Mike applied to join the PGA when he was eighteen and Alex Crombie was one of his sponsors.

Mike vividly recalls one occasion while he was the assistant at Denham when he and Robert Shaw, the actor, played a fourball match against Sean Connery and Donald Steel, the course architect and a member at Denham. Mike and Shaw won on the 18th green when their better ball score was 62 against the 63 of their opponents.

Mike also recalls that it was when he wanted to get married that he had to start looking for a position as professional because it was not easy to do that in those days on an assistant's wage. And it so happened that this was just at the time that the Beaconsfield Club was looking for someone to succeed Alex Crombie. Mike applied for the post and, like the other applicants, who coincidentally included Peter Alliss's son Gary, was interviewed by Harold Staines, Colin Smith and John Woods. Continuing the policy of engaging a club professional rather than a tournament player, they decided to appoint

Professional Mike Brothers, right, with assistant professional Chris Dodds

"the local boy" to the position. In accepting the appointment, Mike agreed to sell Alex's stock for the benefit of his widow and to retain the services of Mike Collet who had been Alex's assistant when he died. In fact, Mike Collet stayed as assistant for several years and when he left Simon Goddard became Mike's assistant for a short while. Chris Dodds, who had previously been at Burton–on–Trent, another Colt designed course, joined Mike in 1985 and he and Mike have now been the professionals at Beaconsfield for a combined total of forty-six years; surely a record for any club?

One of Mike's earliest recollections is of selling club crested pullovers in what was then the Men's Bar because alterations and repairs were being made to the professional's shop at that time – alterations and repairs that, incidentally, necessitated the removal of the fireplace in his shop and the original chimney stack that towered above it. At much the same time, the rules about wide wheel trolleys were introduced and Mike recalls that the sale of replacement wheels became quite a significant part of his business for a time.

Although the job of a club professional has changed considerably since Mike himself was an assistant, the basic task of teaching golf continues much as it has always been, but at Beaconsfield this task became relatively less arduous for the professionals with the development of the driving range and, more recently, with the introduction of the covered bay area – the

113

"penthouse" as it was termed in the first proposal for such a structure many years ago.

Mike was made an Honorary Member of the Club in February 1981 and has now been with the Club for twenty-nine years.

Competitions

"Our big spanish chestnut tries the 'full shoulder turn' when everyone has gone"
by Val Doonican

Rather as happened when the Club first started in the 1920s, the early years of the new members' Club saw several new trophies presented by members or their relatives. These included the Frank Seymour Cup (1954), the Raffety Tankards (1958), the Kelly Salver, the Andrew Wylie Cup and the Whitley-Jones Trophy (all in 1959), the Ellerton Salver (1962) and the Peter Case Trophy (1963). Added to the ones already well established in the fixture list, these new ones provided a full range of trophy competitions in a variety of formats for the various handicap categories. To these trophies were later added the Captain's Dinner Plate donated by George Irving in 1982, the President's Cup donated in 1986 by Colin Paterson M.C. following the completion of his presidency, the Scratch Knock-out Cup presented by Bryan Hines in 1996 and, most recently, the Hamish Paton Quaich donated in 1997 by his wife, Marion, in memory of her husband and a former captain.

A somewhat unusual Stableford competition was held at the new Club on 24th May 1949. Earlier that year, the R&A had written to all affiliated clubs to express its concern at the increasing cost of golf and to suggest that a limitation on the number of clubs that a player was permitted to carry might help to curtail the expenditure. The letter went on to suggest that every club should hold a six clubs and a putter competition and report back the views of its members "so as to get a genuine feel on the question". Beaconsfield duly organised a Stableford competition, but sadly, as so often has been the case, no records were kept to indicate what the Beaconsfield members' views were.

For many years the entrance fee for men's competitions had been 25p and it remained so until the Inland Revenue made a ruling that meant that, as from 1st January 1981, entry fees for golf club competitions would be subject to VAT. The Board took that occasion to double the competition entry fee – from 25p to a staggering 50p!

Captain's Day is a long established event that goes back to the earliest days of the Club after the First World War and by tradition, the format of the competition on that day and the prizes are matters for the captain's choice. In 1932, Sir James Donald was the captain and his Captain's Day prize was a silver cup which, of course, became the winner's property. No more was heard of that cup until almost sixty years later when, in 1990, the winner's son kindly donated the cup to the Club on his father's death. Bill Horgan, who was the captain at the time, presented the cup to the winner of his Captain's Day prize with the intention that he and successive Captain's Day winners should hold it for one year. Although through unawareness, this custom has not been followed every year since then, it was revived in the centenary year and was accordingly presented by Colin Biffa to Graham McCulloch who was the winner of the centenary Captain's Day prize.

The Bloomfield Cup has had a long and curious history. Since it was presented in 1921 it has almost certainly undergone a change of name from "Broomfield" and its format has been changed several times. Even as recently as 1973 the final of the Bloomfield Cup was played as a foursome medal. But there was more change to come. In November 1983, a silver cup was bought from the "Clock Shop" in the Old Town, to be played for in a junior knock-out competition. However, two months later it was noticed that this cup was identical to another one that the Club had purchased sometime earlier as the trophy for the Summer Knock-out competition for five-day members. The Board therefore decided that the twin cups should henceforth be the "Bloomfield Cups" and the secretary was instructed "to look for old cups in the club's possession to see if there are any suitable for the Summer and Junior knock-out competitions". What happened to the original Broomfield Cup has yet to be established. One final curiosity about the twin cups is that they are marked as having been assayed in 1914 – the year that the Beaconsfield Club was established; but that is probably pure coincidence.

Most clubs have some form of Christmas competition and at Beaconsfield it is the Turkey Foursomes which started in 1980, when it was decided that a foursomes Stableford competition open to any combination of male and female members should be held at Christmas time "with perhaps a social after the prize-giving". The prize was to be a turkey for each of the winners and a capon for each of the runners-up. In addition, it was decided that if a lady member was not among the winners or the runners-up, then a prize of two pounds of sausages would be presented to the leading lady or ladies. And so it was that in 1983 when the foursomes partnership of Wendy Gardiner and Mary Stevens returned the leading ladies score, each received two pounds of sausages. For obvious reasons, such a prize was seen to be somewhat inappropriate and in 1986 the leading ladies' prize was changed to a brace of pheasants. By one of those delightful quirks of history, eighteen years later

The Beaconsfield team beat the Oxford University Golf Club at Beaconsfield in 1947 by 4 matches to 2 with 1 halved. Left to right standing: H. G. Collins, "Doc" Ledingham, J. Doherty, Frank Barnes, H. G. W. Davies and H. K. Padfield. Left to right seated: Jack Bracey-Gibbon, Ken Braddon, Lindsay Robertson, Corrie Rissik and Andrew Wylie

that same ladies foursomes partnership, which by then had become part of the tradition of the event, won the 2001 Turkey Foursomes competition and they received their prizes amid great acclamation.

Club Matches

The formation of the new members' Club had little effect on the Club's Fixture List and the men's fixtures against neighbouring clubs have largely remained unchanged to the present day, although some new fixtures have been added.†

In 1990, the Buckinghamshire Scratch League was formed and Beaconsfield joined two years later when Tim Clough was the First Team captain. Although the Club has not yet been able to win the League, under the successive team captaincies of Brad Muir, Douglas Brown and now Richard Clarke, it has at least managed to stay in the first Division. Some non-League First Team matches continue to played against such as the County team and Oxford University and the traditional Good Friday match against

†The development of Ladies, Seniors and Wildebeests matches is dealt with in other Chapters.

the Second Team still takes place. For other fixtures, the Second Team is now designated the "Club Team".

The Club's own England v. Scotland match, first played on 13th May 1961 and followed by what was described as "a social in the Dining Room" is still a keenly contested struggle frequently fought out in the tempests of an English spring whereby the Scottish team gains an unfair advantage. It is very much in keeping with the spirit in which this annual match is played that no records are kept as to how many times each side has won or lost the match – but this may be because recollections tend to become indistinct after "a social in the Dining Room". The victors each year are amply rewarded for their efforts partly through the simple joy of winning and partly by the free wine that is supplied by courtesy of the losing team; on the other hand, the losing team suffers not only the indignity of buying the wine, but also the humiliation of receiving the long wooden spoon that was generously presented to the Club in 1985 by the two team captains for that year, Roger Connor of England and Jim Lawson of Scotland. It has become a commendable characteristic of this match in recent times that the Scottish selection committee has been prepared to recognise the playing qualifications of Welsh and Irish nationals and, indeed, those of other nationals as the need arises.

The Club's annual match against the Royal Army Educational Corps is one that recalls its historic links with Wilton Park. For all practical purposes, the death of Colonel Du Pre and the Club's purchase of the freehold marked the end of the long association between the Club and Wilton Park. But it was a separation that was not to last long for, by another curious quirk of history, connections between the Club and Wilton Park were to be restored when the Army School of Education was moved from Bodmin to Wilton Park in 1951, and the Club granted affiliated membership for up to eight officers and twelve other ranks of the RAEC stationed at Wilton Park. Soon after this affiliation had been established, matches between the Club and the Corps began to be played and have continued almost every year since, with each side hosting the dinner following the match in alternate years either at the clubhouse or in the Officers Mess at Wilton Park. Since 1970, the winning team receives the Long John Thomas Trophy, a tankard so named after its three donors, namely Neville *Long*, Major *John* Burch and Brigadier Harry *Thomas*. The credit for contriving this name goes to Walter Gutteridge, the organiser of the Club's team for this match, and the embarrassment of explaining to a young female assistant how the names were to be engraved on the tankard so as to bring out the name of the trophy went to Harry Thomas.

Because of the declining number of RAEC personnel at Wilton Park, the affiliated membership was ended in 1993 and the few existing Wilton Park members were transferred to the Club's Temporary Membership category, which continues to be available should there be appropriate Wilton Park staff in the future. The annual match continues to be played, but its continuance must depend to a large extent on the future of the army at Wilton Park.

Course Records

The Professional Record

Curiously, the first mention of a course record at Beaconsfield appears not in any of the Club's own documents, but in *The Sunday Times* issue for 13th February 1921 where it is reported that an unattached professional named C. McIlvenney scored 69 on two consecutive days against a "bogey" of 76 and that this score was the professional record for the course. The reporter adds that the second round would have been better had McIlvenney not had a 6 at the 6th hole.

Like most records, however, this one was set only to be broken and so it was by the Club's own professional, James Jones, who is recorded in *The Golfer's Handbook* for 1922 as then being the holder of the professional record with a score of 66.

One of the difficulties that inevitably arises in connection with course records is that courses change over the years and this makes it difficult to determine when a new record has been established. At Beaconsfield, because of changes to the course, Percy Alliss' record of 62 (*The Golfer's Handbook* for 1952) was replaced as the professional course record by the 63 scored by Ewen Murray in the 1981 Pro-Am competition. In turn, Murray's record was itself replaced by the two 65s returned by Bill Longmuir and Paul Stewart, both from The London Golf Club, in the Centenary Year Pro-Am. Those two scores now stand as the Club's professional record.

The Amateur Record

The earliest reference to an amateur record that has so far been traced is in a Board minute in 1949. It appears that in the Captain's Day Stableford competition that year, Ken Braddon returned a score of 42 points having been round in 68 strokes which was two strokes better than the existing amateur record of 70 held jointly by Ken himself and Corrie Rissik. The question then arose as to whether Ken's 68 could be regarded as a new record since it was not scored in a medal round. Having consulted the definition of a "course record" in the then current edition of *The Golfer's Handbook*, the Board came to the conclusion that Ken's 68 "could only count as an unofficial record and that Mr. Braddon should be so informed".

Pamela Davies (Griffiths) winner of the Girls British Open Amateur Championship Cup which she won at Beaconsfield in 1949 beating Arlette Jaquet (Belgium) in the final

In 1966, the Board decided that there should be two amateur records, namely a "Members' Record" and an "Open Record" and that the cards of both should be exhibited in the clubhouse. For that reason, the 70 that Richard Ling had returned in a competition that year was regarded as a new Members' Record because the course had changed sufficiently. The Open Record at that time appears to have been by held by a Mr. Warren.

In the September 1969 Monthly Medal, Don McIntosh returned a score of 69 which became "the Members' Record for the re-constructed course" and his card was duly exhibited.

In the second round of the English Golf Union's Champion Club Tournament held at Beaconsfield in 1988, Mr. D. Haines, a member of the team representing Burnham & Berrow Golf Club, returned a score of 66 which became and still remains the Open Record for the course. As it happened, Haines's card was marked by Ian Wheater who was the club champion at the time.

It is most pleasing to note that the Members' Record is now shared by two former junior members of the Club, Robert Christian and Richard Clarke both of whom have returned a score of 67. Robert returned that score twice in 2001 – once in the course of winning the Club Championship that year – and Richard scored his 67 in the second round on his way to winning the Club Championship in the centenary year.

Vesey Rafferty, captain of the club, presents the British Girls Open Amateur Championship Cup to Angela Ward, later Angela Bonnallack, 1955

Notable Golfing Events

By the time of his death in 1946, Colonel Du Pre's efforts to establish Beaconsfield well and truly on the golfing map had been remarkably successful. Exhibition matches by top class professionals, and leading amateur tournaments such as the Golf Illustrated Golf Vase, had been held at Beaconsfield before the war and it was a Club and course of considerable standing that the members purchased in 1948. The continuation of this standing by the new Club brought several more significant golfing events to Beaconsfield.

Even as early as 1948, the Board of the new Club granted the LGU's request to hold the Girls Championship and the Girls International Team Cup at Beaconsfield in September the following year. Pamela Davies (Griffiths) won the Championship and also captained the Welsh Girls team in the international tournament that was held at Beaconsfield the next day. Pamela herself went on to represent Wales in the Home Internationals from 1965 to 1971 and to achieve many other golfing honours. The success of that event brought the Girls Championship back to Beaconsfield in 1955 when the winner was Angela Ward (now Mrs. Bonnallack) who played in the Curtis Cup Match the following year and on six other occasions. Enclosed with the LGU's letter of appreciation to the Club after that particular event was a £10 gratuity for the Club's staff which the Board divided "equally between the indoor and outdoor staff". The Girls Championship returned to the Club again in 1962.

The secretary of the Lord Roberts Workshop wrote to the Club in 1951 seeking permission to use the course the following year for a charity exhibition match between top professionals. The Board not only agreed, but also instructed the Green Committee to offer every assistance in the organisation of the event. In the Club's files there is an undated photograph taken about this same time of four professionals on the first tee at Beaconsfield. The four professionals, who are obviously taking part in an exhibition match, are Percy Alliss, Bill Cox, Bob Kenyon and Henry Cotton.

An exhibition match at Beaconsfield probably in 1951
Left to right: Percy Alliss, Bill Cox, Bob Kenyon and Henry Cotton

Whether this photograph was taken on the occasion of the Lord Roberts Workshop exhibition match or some other exhibition match at the Club has not yet been ascertained, but it is interesting to note the local affiliations of the four professionals. Alliss and Kenyon had both been professionals at Beaconsfield, Cox had been born in Chalfont St Giles, had been an assistant professional at Beaconsfield and professional at Gerrards Cross, and Henry Cotton was professional at Ashridge and then at Temple. This initial contact between the Lord Roberts Workshop and the Club may well have been the origin of the annual mixed foursomes competition played under that name at the Club on Easter Mondays.

Other notable events of national as opposed to county or regional significance held at Beaconsfield include, in addition to the EGU Champion Club Tournament mentioned above, the ELGA Intermediate Championship in 1994 and the Golf Foundation Team Championship for Schools in 1996. There is no doubt that many other golfing events could have been held at Beaconsfield had the Board so wished, but the Board has always been mindful of the needs of its members. Thus, for example, when in 1983 the Women Professional Golfers Association made enquiries about holding the White Horse Whiskey tournament at Beaconsfield, the request was turned down, as the captain, Richard Zeidler, explained at the next AGM, "on account of the disruption that would be caused to members playing in mid-week."

121

Lt. Colonel Taylor and Peter Chase, Official starters at the 1960 Pro-Am

The Pro-Ams

In the hundred years of its existence, no single day has seen more golfing talent on display at Beaconsfield than Saturday 26th April 1958, the day of the first "Professional and Amateur Invitation Foursomes". Such events were largely unknown at that time and it may be that the one at Beaconsfield was one of the first to be held. It was Gordon Le Mare, the father of Robert who himself has been a member of the Club since 1955, who suggested to the Board in 1957 that it would be "beneficial to the Club" to hold such an event and that an appropriate day would be the day after the end of the Spalding Tournament at Moor Park the following year. That suggestion was taken up and a Competition Committee, chaired by the captain, Douglas Gordon, was established. The event differed from the format of current Pro-Ams in that each team consisted of only two players, one of whom was a professional. With the amateurs' handicaps limited to 9, one hundred and twenty competitors took part and among the sixty professionals who participated were six of the Ryder Cup team that had been successful in beating the American team at Lindrick the year before; they were Peter Alliss, Ken Bousfield, Harry Bradshaw, Max Faulkner, Bernard Hunt, Peter Mills and Christy O'Connor Snr. In addition to these, nine former and three future Ryder Cup players also took part. Gordon Le Mare himself partnered Harry Bradshaw

122

Jimmy Hume, assistant professional at Beaconsfield, driving at the 1st in the 1960 Pro-Am

Max Faulkner (centre player) watches one of his team putt on the 16th green in the 1960 Pro-Am

George Irving, captain, presents the team trophy to Ewen Murray at the 1981 Pro-Am. Ewen Murray returned the professional record score of 63

while the Club's own professional, Alex Crombie, partnered Lindsay Robertson.

The weather on the day could hardly have been worse with rain and a strong wind not only affecting the players but also marring spectator attendance. Nevertheless, it was considered a great success and the competition was most fittingly won by Peter Alliss and his partner, Harold Ridgeley, with a thirty-six hole net (and gross) total of 140. The beneficial part of the day for the Club came not only in the press coverage, but also in the form of much needed income; even apart from the profit on bar sales, the final accounts showed a profit of £50.12s. on the event. Moreover, the sweepstake, conducted this time in full accord with The Small Lotteries and Gaming Act, contributed over £250.

Such was the success of this first Pro-Am that it was decided to hold a similar event in the same format the following April. Although the number of entries was down, the Starting Sheet shows that most of the same past and future Ryder Cup players took part again. This time, Alex Crombie was partnered by Harold Staines. Unfortunately, the weather was even worse than it had been the year before and this probably explains why the balance sheet showed a loss of some £34; but happily, as the Board recorded, "the profit on bar sales was £50".

Despite bar profits, an overall loss was made on the Pro-Am in 1960 and the Board decided that, rather than make it an annual event, it should be left to each Board in the future to decide for itself whether or not to hold such a competition.

The Club's next foray into this type of event did not take place until August 1981 when a competition in the current Pro-Am format of one professional and three amateurs was held in support of The Golf Foundation. One hundred and seventy-two competitors took part with George Irving, the captain, partnering Barry Lane while Mike Brothers was teamed with three members of Beaconsfield namely, Richard Zeidler, John Burch and Bob Hornall. Again, the event was very successful and

George Irving receives the Golf Foundation Gus Payne Trophy from Michael Bonnallack in 1982.
Mike Hunter, the secretary, is on the right

the net surplus enabled a cheque for £1,120 to be presented to the Foundation. It was in this Pro-Am that Ewen Murray, then the professional at Walton Heath, returned a score of 63 which became the new professional record for the course. Similar Pro-Ams in support of The Golf Foundation were held into the mid-1980s and many of the amateurs who took part in them are still members of the Club and have vivid memories of those events. At a ceremony after the 1982 Pro-Am, Michael Bonnallack, on behalf of the Foundation, presented the Club with the Gus Payne Trophy which is awarded each year to the Club making the highest single contribution to the Foundation's annual appeal.

There were no more such competitions until the Centenary Pro-Am in July 2002 organised as part of the centenary year celebrations by a Committee of Douglas Brown, the vice-captain as chairman, Sue Edwards, Hugh Evans and Graham Collins who, as well as being a member of the Club, is the Tournament Controller of the PGA Southern Region. Their efforts produced an entry of two hundred competitors – the largest for any of the Club's Pro-Ams – and enabled a substantial cheque to be given to the captain's charity, the Iain Rennie Hospice at Home. The winning team was David Mills, the professional at Seaford, two members, Ralph Findlay and Julie Cooper, and a guest, Caroline Harden. Coincidentally, the two professionals from The London Golf Club, Bill Longmuir and Paul Stuart,

The centenary Pro-Am winning team with the ladies captain. Left to right: David Mills, professional at Seaford Golf Club, Julie Cooper, Judy Gill, ladies captain, Caroline Harden and Ralph Findlay

both returned a score of 65 to share the professionals' first prize and, because significant changes had been made to the course since Ewen Murray's 63 in 1981, these scores have been recognised as the new professional record for the course.

Golf Fanatics International

Through its own competitions and by making its facilities available, Beaconsfield, like many other golf clubs, has contributed substantially over the years to local and national charities such as the Red Cross, the NSPCC, the Abbeyfield, Cancer Research, the RNLI and so on.

Golf Fanatics International is one such charitable organisation that has been holding a golf day at Beaconsfield for a quarter of a century. Taking as its precept that "A man is never so tall as when he stoops to help a child", the GFI raises money to buy wheelchairs for disabled children and has so far provided well over a hundred such chairs. Founded in 1975, its first meeting was staged at the East Devon Golf Club in Budleigh Salterton and it came to Beaconsfield for the first time two years later – probably because one of the Club's newest members at that time just happened to be the captain of the GFI. His name was Val Doonican.

Val still remembers with pleasure the hospitality with which they were received and the wonderful support that was given by the artisans who offered their services as caddies.

Members' Golfing Achievements

Achievement is a relative concept and while the achievements of several members are related elsewhere, sadly those of others can find no place. But all of them are important if only to those involved and recounting here a few individual achievements is not in any way to diminish the significance of those of other members.

The London Amateur Foursomes

The London Amateur Foursomes competition is one of the oldest and most prestigious amateur scratch tournaments in the south of England. It started in 1907 and is open to teams from any club that has at least one green within a forty mile radius of Charing Cross. The first recorded entry of a team from Beaconsfield was in October 1947 when the tournament was held at West Hill, but the records do not indicate who were in the Beaconsfield team. The Club entered one and sometimes two teams for several years after that and two particularly strong teams were entered in 1961; they were Ken Braddon and his son Richard and Jack Bracey-Gibbon and Lindsay Robertson. However, success in the event for a Beaconsfield team did not come until 1978 when the event was played at Moor Park and was won by Roger Ames and Ian Wheater – still the only left-handed pair to have won this tournament. This success was repeated for the Club in 1987 by the team of Freddie George and David Lewis when the tournament was again held at Moor Park.

That year was a particularly successful year for Freddie George who emerged, under the watchful eyes of Mike Brothers and Chris Dodds, from the ranks of the Club's junior members to be one of the country's leading amateur golfers. Having been Club champion in 1982, Freddie became a member of the England Boys International Team in 1983 and the England Youth International Team the following year. His amateur career came to a peak in 1987 when, as well as winning the London Foursomes with David Lewis, the Berkhamsted Trophy and the BB&O County Championship, he became a full English International and also qualified to play in the Open at Muirfield. That is a considerable achievement for any amateur, but Freddie had the added distinction of being the very first player to tee off in the Open that year. He became a professional golfer in 1988 and, having been an assistant at Gerrards Cross, is now the professional at the North Middlesex Club.

127

Golfing Marathons

Although golf is not a game where endurance in the ordinary sense in which the term is employed in sport is required, there are several instances of feats of endurance on the links which demanded great physical extension.

Reg Rundle celebrates his 100 holes of golf in a day on his sixtieth birthday, 1992

It is with these words that the R&A introduces the section on Feats of Endurance in *The Golfer's Handbook* and while for many of us completing eighteen holes is often a feat of endurance, that is of nothing compared to two feats that have been recorded at Beaconsfield.

Under the heading "Golfer does six rounds in a day", the *Daily Mail* reported a bet that Tom Piggot, an 18 handicapper aged twenty-five of Courtfield Gardens, London, made with Norman Cosgrave that for £15 he could play six rounds of golf (108 holes) at Beaconsfield in a day. That was in September 1955 and, starting at 4.30 a.m. and carrying only three clubs, he won his bet just as darkness was falling at 8 p.m. As he looked at his blistered feet and reached yet again for the surgical spirit, Tom was reported to have commented, "I don't play much golf and this was an interesting experience." Norman Cosgrave was a member of the Club from 1949 to 1958 and it seems probable that Tom Piggot was also a member, but no record of this has yet been found.

But what the young can do, the more mature golfer can sometimes match – or nearly match. Sunday August 2nd 1992 was the sixtieth birthday of Reg Rundle who had by then been a member of the Club for just over a quarter of a century. As he stood there on the 1st tee at 5.10 a.m. that morning with his wife, Susan, as his first marker of the day, he may perhaps have been forgiven for having doubts about the wisdom of his decision to seek the Board's permission to play 100 holes in a day for charity. But there was no going back now and, armed with seven clubs and a putter and with the co-operation of other players out on the course later in the day, he successfully concluded his mission at 7.55 p.m. He maintains that he would have finished earlier had the captain, Hamish Paton, not insisted on buying him a drink but, as Reg says, "To disappoint a Scot who offers to buy you a drink would have been unkind." He still recalls the challenging words of the assistant steward as he set off at seven o'clock in the evening for the last ten holes, "Don't forget, Sir, the bar closes at eight o'clock on Sundays." The champagne was served with five minutes to spare! After 492 strokes and 100 holes, the Special Baby Unit at High Wycombe Hospital and the South Bucks Association for the Disabled were each £400 better off. A great achievement indeed, but Reg is seventy in this centenary year and who knows what greater feats he may yet attempt?

Golfing Blues

Over the years, several members of the Club have been Oxford or Cambridge Blues for golf. One such member, Ian Wheater, who was Club champion for ten consecutive years from 1972 and who won the Championship on two other occasions, received three Blues for golf at Oxford and went on to win the President's Putter in 1959 and again in 1961.

What may well be a record for any golf club occurred in the Oxford v. Cambridge match played at Saunton, North Devon, in 1973, for no less than three of the participants were members of Beaconsfield at the time. Two of them, Kevin Garnett and Tom Hawes, played for Oxford while the third, Ian Pattinson, was captain of the Cambridge team. Kevin lost both his singles and his foursomes, Tom won both his singles and his foursomes and Ian lost his singles and halved his foursomes. Tom is the son of Cliff Hawes who has been a member of the Club since 1968.

And Other Achievements

Playing in the inaugural Rosebery Cup, an open amateur event, at Ashridge in July 1933, a member of Beaconsfield, E. H. Chambers, returned a remarkable score of 65 in the morning round. Unfortunately, his score of 80 in the afternoon – "following a premature celebration at the bar" – prevented his winning the cup although he managed to finish third some five strokes behind.

It is clear from the Hole-in-One Book on display in the Members' Room that many members have already mastered the technique of scoring aces. Joyce Braddon obviously brought this technique to perfection, at least as regards the 16th hole, where she had the distinction of scoring a hole-in-one no less than five times. Commenting after her fifth ace which she achieved in a ladies' medal competition, Joyce acknowledged that it was "all a matter of luck", but admitted that while the first three needed a 6-iron, the last two needed a 5-wood due to advancing maturity.

Similarly, Judith Goodwyn has the distinction, unique for the Club so far as can be discovered, of having had an ace on all four short holes – and all within the space of fourteen months. A truly remarkable achievement.

Ian Harris, club champion in 1951 and 1953, also won the BB&O County Championship in 1953 at Fritford Heath

Past Captains Annual Dinner, 2002
Back row left to right: Ken Kingshott, Mike Wisdom, Bob Sutton, Roger Crabb, Douglas Brown (vice-captaon), Ken Robertson, Jim Lawson, Gordon Bull, Allan Robertson, Bill Horgan.
Seated left to right: Colin Smith, Alan Neale, Bryan Hines,† Derek Randall,† Colin Biffa (captain), Roger Connor (president), Alistair Hamilton,† George Irving, Gordon Tuck
†Past presidents

The Captain, Colin Biffa, the Ladies Captain, Judy Gill and the President, Roger Connor, at the Centenary Ball

Bill Bryce (left), President of the English Golf Union presents the EGU's Centenary Plate to Douglas Brown, vice-captain of Beaconsfield Golf Club at the BB&O Annual Dinner in 2002

Family Fun Day

The clown – or is it Sally Darby? – at the Family Fun Day

Fourth generation: Tiger Beck, great grandson of David and Joan Ellis, holes out at the 6th

Rob Lucas, chairman of the Social Committee, at the Family Fun Day

The fly agaric fungus

Peacock butterfly feeding on thistles

Chapter Twelve

The Ladies' Section

Mr. Johnston, having described the various phases of the contest, proceeded to read the results of the ladies' competition, in which Miss E. O. Hill and Miss L. Anketell secured first and second place respectively. Sir John Aird then presented Miss Hill with the first prize, consisting of a handsome silver clock and thermometer combined. The second prize, an elegant chatelaine and case, was handed to Miss Anketell. Mr. Johnston then announced the result of the competition for the gentlemen's prizes …

Although very little is known about the Wilton Park Club, this extract from the *South Bucks Free Press* reporting the Club's first known prize giving event in May 1907 clearly shows that, from the beginning, men and women have shared a common history of golf at Beaconsfield.

Several, if not most, of the members of the Wilton Park Club are known to have transferred to the new Beaconsfield Club when it opened in 1914 and among the lady members that did so were Mrs. J. Bailey-Gibson, the wife of a local solicitor, and Mrs. Commeline, the wife of the rector of Beaconsfield, the Rev. A. S. Commeline. They were the winner and runner-up in the ladies' competition held at the Wilton Park Club in 1912.

It was in May 1919 that the acting secretary of the new Club, George Langley-Taylor, wrote to a Mrs. Herbert Tilley, at 72, Harley Street, W1, in connection with the Club's becoming a member of the Ladies Golf Union. In his customarily curt style, he wrote:

Madam,

Miss Cecil Leitch has proposed the Club for membership of the Ladies Golf Union. We have to be proposed and seconded by members of a club that is at present affiliated to the LGU. Miss Leitch has given me your name as a seconder. Will you kindly do this by signing the enclosed and returning it to me.

The enclosed application form was duly signed and returned, and in June 1919 Beaconsfield Golf Club was admitted to membership of the LGU on payment of three guineas "to cover the entrance fee and the first annual subscription".

Cecil Leitch, who was probably a member of the Club by this time and to whom further reference is made in Chapter Fourteen, was one of the outstanding women golfers of the time and a minute of the Club's General Committee the following month recorded that "Miss Cecil Leitch had been elected Lady Captain". That minute, however, appears to have been somewhat premature because a fortnight later the secretary found himself reporting to the Committee that Miss Leitch had written to say that she was "not able to accept the position of Ladies' captain". The Committee then decided to invite Mrs. Herbert Tilley, who had only recently seconded the Club's application to become a member of the LGU, to become the Ladies' captain, but unfortunately, she also was unable to accept.

The lady members were obviously not too pleased at still not having a Ladies' captain and, in August, wrote to the Committee expressing their concern over this and also asking about the formation of a Ladies' committee. The secretary was instructed to advise them that a Ladies' captain would be appointed in due course and that, while no formal ladies' committee could be recognised, the ladies were free to set up an informal committee if they wished and that they could be assured that any suggestions that such a committee might choose to make would be sympathetically considered. It seems probable that Colonel Du Pre had originally had it in mind to appoint a leading lady golfer as the Ladies' captain to enhance the Club's prestige, but this obviously proved rather more difficult than had been expected and it was only two months later that it was decided that the secretary should "arrange for the lady members to elect their own captain". The ladies were thus able to go ahead and establish an "informal" Ladies' Committee which met for the first time on 5th March 1920. It was at that meeting that Mrs. Evelyn Wood was elected as the first Ladies' captain of Beaconsfield Golf Club and Mrs. Woozley was elected the first honorary secretary of the Ladies' section. Mrs. Wood was followed as Ladies' captain by Mrs. Beecroft in 1921, Mrs. Harvey in 1922 and Mrs. Gavin in 1923.

Mrs. Gavin's captaincy is somewhat mysterious. Born into an aristocratic family in 1884 as Evelyn Ryder, she became an accomplished golfer and was an English international player by 1910. Before the First World War she had been a member of several clubs west of London including Burnham Beeches and Huntercombe, but during the war she lived mostly in America where she was runner-up in the Women's Championship in 1915, 1919 and 1922. She became a member of Beaconsfield in May 1922 and her husband joined a month later. There is a record of her playing in the top match for the ladies away match against Harewood Downs within a few days of her becoming a member; she won her match by 6 and 5 and the team won by $4^1/2$ matches to $3^1/2$. Later that year she and Mrs. Brindle were nominated to represent the Club in the London Ladies Foursomes to be held at Addington and she was also invited to become Ladies' captain.

At the ensuing AGM of the Ladies' section, she was duly elected Ladies' captain for 1923-1924. She was not actually present at that meeting, but sent a letter to say how much she appreciated the honour and how much she regretted that "a very serious operation prevented her attending the meeting". There are records of two meetings of the Ladies' committee during Mrs. Gavin's year of office but she did not attend either of them and so her predecessor, Mrs. Harvey, chaired them. What is perhaps most remarkable is that in the minutes of neither meeting is there a reference to Mrs. Gavin nor is she recorded as having sent apologies for absence. Mrs. Rissik succeeded her as Ladies' captain at the next AGM – but still no mention of Mrs. Gavin. In 1925, Mrs. Gavin played in the British Women's Championship at Troon having entered as a member of Huntercombe, and, as she recalls in her book, *A Gallery of Women Golfers,* Enid Wilson was defeated that year in the first round by Mrs. Gavin. The following year, Mrs. Gavin's entry form for the same championship shows her as having entered as a member of Beaconsfield. She later married C. V. L. Hooman who had been a Walker Cup player in 1922-1923. It is a most intriguing episode in the history of the Club.

Cecil Leitch, who had declined the invitation to become the first Ladies' captain, returned to Beaconsfield in May 1937 to present the prizes at the "Overseas Ladies Invitation Meeting" that LGU had organised for the large number of its members from the Dominions and Colonies who were coming to London for the Coronation of King Edward VIII. Having given its approval for the LGU to hold this event at Beaconsfield, the Committee presented a silver rose bowl to the LGU as the prize for the competition. The LGU Executive Council minutes relating to that event record that there was a visitors' competition in the morning at which "famous British golfers acted as hostesses and the prizes were given away by Miss Cecil Leitch" and that "in the afternoon there was an exhibition match in which Miss Pam Barton and Mrs. Holm played Mrs. Wanda Morgan and Miss Enid Wilson".

Membership of the Ladies' Section

For some unknown reason, the election of ladies to Full membership of the Club had been suspended by the Club's Committee during the First World War and for a short while afterwards but, in October 1919, it was decided to lift the suspension until such time as the total number reached 100. If attendance at the AGM of the Ladies' section in 1921 is anything to go by, the number of lady members at that time was probably much below that figure, for only the Ladies' captain and fifteen other members were present. Nevertheless, two years later, the upper limit was raised to 125 for Full

---

†"Qualified" membership seems to have been a category of five-day membership open to those (males or females) who had previously been full members and who, by paying an additional subscription, had the right to play at weekends on payment of the specified green fee. In 1929 the subscription for such a member was six guineas.

membership and to twenty-five for Qualified† and Five-day membership. The Qualified membership later disappeared and the upper limits have subsequently been revised on several occasions.

It is somewhat surprising that, even as late as 1970, the procedure for approving female applicants for membership was, and very probably always had been, the same as that for men. In other words, neither the Ladies' Committee nor the Ladies' captain was involved in the approval procedure – at least not until Mrs. Helen Brown became the Ladies' captain in 1969. Being as she said, "very alarmed" at such a situation, she took the matter up with the Board and was able to report to a meeting of the Ladies' Committee early the following year that she had managed to obtain an assurance that, in future, the name of each new lady applicant would be referred to the Ladies' Committee before any final decision was taken. This, she said, would enable the ladies "to judge their suitability over a cup of coffee or a few holes". Two years later, the Ladies' Committee decided that before any new lady member was admitted she must be interviewed by members of the Ladies' Committee and that her admission would depend largely on golfing ability and knowledge of the game – in contrast, presumably, to what had previously been the case.

It was a specific rule of the original Beaconsfield Club that "Lady members shall not have any power in the management of the Club" and therefore it is not at all surprising that there was no lady member on its Board nor is there any record of one being invited to be a member of its General Committee. That discrimination did not find its way into the members company that was formed in 1948 and, in fact, two lady members, Florence "Bunty" Duncan and Nancye Gold, were elected to the first Board of the new Club.

"Ladies Day"

The practice of lady members being allocated a weekday on which to play their competitions goes back, of course, to the days when, generally speaking, the men were at work during the week while the ladies stayed at home.

At Beaconsfield, the day originally set aside as "ladies medal day" was Tuesday, but at the Club's AGM in 1925, the day was changed to Thursday because it had been discovered that "there was a cheap train fare from town" on that day.

Thursday remained Ladies Day at Beaconsfield until 1961 when the captain, Charles Crockwell, persuaded the Board that "it would be more practical for Tuesdays to be allotted in future for Competitions, etc., organised by the Ladies' section instead of alternate Thursdays as at present." This remark was apparently made in the context of a letter that had been received from the Ladies' section asking that in the following year, 1962, every Thursday in the month, as opposed to the first and second Thursdays only, should be kept free of golfing societies so that ladies would be able to play their increasing number of competitions. The Board, however, was not at all favourable to that suggestion because experience showed that golfing societies, upon whom the Club still depended for a substantial proportion of its income, preferred Wednesdays or Thursdays. Moreover, several of the Club's house staff had Tuesdays off and so for that additional reason Tuesdays were not suitable for societies. The Board therefore responded that if the ladies would change from Thursdays to Tuesdays, they could have every Tuesday, but if they wanted to retain Thursdays they would have to let the Board know well in advance which extra Thursdays they would like to have so as to avoid Societies being arranged for those days.

The Ladies' Committee intended to discuss this response at their next AGM, but before that took place they received a short and surprising letter from Colonel Dean, the secretary, which read:

> In order to assist in the general administration of the club, the Directors have placed Tuesdays at the disposal of your Committee for Club competitions, matches, etc. in the future instead of alternate Thursdays as in the past. They hope this will not cause your Committee any appreciable inconvenience. Will you let me know in due course if there is any Tuesday in 1962 that you will not require.

The tone and somewhat peremptory nature of this letter caused "a lot of discussion and a certain amount of disagreement" at the Ladies' Committee on 12th October, and there was as "a strong view that for a very long time the ladies had played their competitions on Thursdays and the whole rhythm of their week had been centred on Thursdays being a day of golf and a change would mean an upheaval in certain individual homes". Nevertheless, at the ladies' AGM it was eventually decided by 22 votes to 11 that the ladies would give Tuesdays a trial for twelve months on the basis that, at the end of that time, the Board would be prepared to review the situation. The incoming Ladies' Captain, Ann Burgess, wrote to the Board to this effect and the Board agreed to the trial period. What, if any, conclusions were drawn from the trial is not recorded, but the following September Colonel Dean wrote to the Ladies' Committee to say that, as from 1963, Ladies Day would revert to Thursdays and that "priority would be given to competitions between 12 noon and 2 p.m." Clarification of this latter point revealed that it meant that there were no restrictions on ladies playing before 12 noon or after 2 p.m. if they wanted to do so.

That remained the position until 1973 when the captain, Dick Edwards, suggested that the ladies might prefer to have the 1st tee reserved for them each Thursday for a fixed period in the morning and again in the afternoon. This was agreed, but with the increasing number of ladies playing on

Thursdays, said to be about eighty on average in 1982, the actual reserved times had to be changed periodically. Further discussions in 1982 led the Green Committee to recommend that the reserved tee times should be "nominally amended" so as to consist of one period only from 9.00 a.m. to 1.00 p.m. This approach of having a single, continuous period of reserved 1st tee time together with the adoption by the Ladies' section of starting-time sheets proved altogether more efficient in the changing circumstances and is the basis of the position today.

Restrictions on Playing Times

Either by rule or by convention, restrictions on playing times at weekends and on public holidays have been additional limitations that lady members have usually encountered in the older, traditional golf clubs. And so it was at Beaconsfield where the Club's rules specifically authorised the making of such restrictions: "The Committee shall have power from time to time, as they think necessary, to make, alter, and vary Regulations and Bye-laws restricting the play of Lady Members."

Current members have no recollection of any such restrictions being put into writing and it is doubtful whether any such regulations or bye-laws were ever made. Nevertheless, there was a long established "custom" that, unless they had been granted special dispensation by the secretary, lady members did not play at weekends and public holidays until after 11 a.m. and then only provided that no men's competition was being played. This custom seems also to have applied even if the lady member was playing with her husband, for at a Ladies' Committee meeting in November 1968, Joan Ellis, the Ladies' Captain, felt it necessary to warn about "murmurings among the men" regarding ladies playing with their husbands at "inconvenient times" at week-ends, and she went on to suggest that, in order to avoid a complete ban on their playing at week-ends, the ladies needed to be "extra careful". At the ladies' AGM the following year, her successor, Helen Brown, referred to the "usual grumbles about week-end play" and went on forcibly to remind the ladies that "they paid less subs than the men and that they must play fair and not get in the way on Saturdays and Sundays".

In return for "accepting" playing restrictions such as these, lady members in most clubs have traditionally paid reduced subscriptions, but increasingly these anomalies are being phased out as they have now been at Beaconsfield.

In the context of reduced subscriptions, it should also be mentioned that, as in most of the older clubs, not only were the ladies subject to playing restrictions, but the running of the Ladies' section, including the organisation of their competitions, inter-club matches and other functions, had been almost entirely in the hands of their Committee and members.

139

There had been minimum imposition on the Club's secretariat. With the recent equalisation of subscriptions, some of the financial and administrative functions of the Ladies' section are now being transferred to the secretariat.

In the context of "equalisation", it has also to be mentioned that the last bastion of male preserve in golf clubs, the "Men's Bar", is now also a thing of the past at Beaconsfield. It is now the "Members Bar". Originally, it was an exclusively male domain, but with the passage of time, exceptions came to be made and it was in order to clarify the somewhat confused situation that had developed that, in 1983, the Board, "without wishing to make a hard and fast rule", issued a guideline to the steward. This was to the effect that, while ladies may use the Men's Bar at all social functions, they would be permitted to use the Bar at other times provided that they were accompanied by a male member and that any other male members in the Bar at the time were "in accord". That guidance was subsequently changed so that ladies were also allowed in the Men's Bar after 6 p.m. whether or not accompanied by a male member. Happily, all that has now become history.

Competitions

At its very first meeting held on 5th March 1920, the "informal" Ladies' Committee decided that there should be a medal competition on the first Tuesday and a bogey competition on the third Tuesday of each month. In addition, they agreed to ask the Club Committee for permission to hold Spring and Autumn Meetings on dates that would be agreed with the club, and it was further agreed to "invite Mrs. Newcombe down from the LGU with a view to altering the ladies "par" for the course".

The first Spring Meeting was held on 4th June that year and the first Autumn Meeting in October. Both meetings were one day events. A certain Miss Young was clearly in good form that year because she won the morning medal competition at the Spring Meeting with a net score of 83 (105-22) and the "approaching and putting" competition in the afternoon. Her winning form continued at the Autumn Meeting despite a reduction in handicap for, as the *Daily Mail* reported, she was the winner of Division 1 with a net score of 79 (99-20). Divison 2 was won by Mrs. Sutton with a net 78 playing off 27.

The second Autumn Meeting was a two day event held on 14th and 15th October 1921. On the first day there was a medal competition in the morning and a foursomes competition in the afternoon. The second day was given over to a "bogey round" in the morning followed in the afternoon by a nine hole one club competition, a long driving competition and a putting competition. The prizes, which were donated by various lady members, included £1 gift vouchers to be spent in the professional's shop, six Silver King golf balls, a writing case and a silver spoon. On this occasion, the Club

Oct: 14th	*One Club Competition 9 holes*		
afternoon	Miss Martelli	51–10	= 41
	Miss Young	56–10	= 46
	Mrs Wood	61–15	= 46
	Mrs Baker	57–10½	= 46½
	Mrs Brindle	51–3	= 48
	Miss Comale	55–7	= 49
	Mrs Tatham	56–7	= 49
	Miss Crowe	60–10	= 50
	Mrs Harvey	58–7½	= 50½
	Mrs Handon	67–14	53
	Miss Cresey	60–6½	= 53½
	Mrs Dredge	67–13	= 54
	Mrs Gardner	72–18	= 54
	Mrs Padfield	69–13½	= 55½
	Driving Competition		
	Mrs Padfield	165 yards	
	Mrs Saunders	163 yards	
	Putting Competition 18 holes		
	Mrs Handon	41	
	Mrs Ralph	44	
	Mrs Dredge	45	

Result of the afternoon competitions held on the second day of the 1921 autumn meeting

Committee had allowed each lady member who competed in the meeting to invite a guest to participate without payment of a green fee. The results sheet for the second day shows that the long driving competition was won by Mrs. Padfield with a drive of 165 yards.

The Spring and Autumn Meetings are still principal events on the ladies' fixture list, although by 1938, instead of being four rounds over two days, they had become one day events, and they remained so until 2001 when the Spring Meeting was changed to a one round competition on each of two consecutive days – a format that has been retained for 2002.

Probably the earliest of the named trophies in the Ladies' section was The Artisans Cup, which was presented by the Artisans Golfing Society (as it was then called) in October 1927. The Ladies' section responded to this "most warmly appreciated" gesture by donating a prize for the artisans to play for in their Spring Meeting. This prize was most likely the "Silver Cigarette Case presented by the Beaconsfield Ladies Golf Club … won by E. C. Berry" (minute of the Artisans Special General Meeting, August 1928). Except for the war years, the Artisans Cup has been played for annually ever since.

Since those early days, many named trophies have been donated to the Ladies' section and several of them have a mini-history of their own. There

141

1928
Beaconsfield Ladies & Artisans Mixed Foursome
Medal Competition Wed: Sept 26th
Played on 1/2 combined handicap
Order of Play

1	Miss Hale 12	Mrs Hutton 14
	Mr Berry Sc	Mr Watson 16
2	Miss Finch 15	Mrs Hutchinson 20
	Mr Newton 17	Mr Child 17
3	Mrs Harvey 21	Mrs Handon 18
	Mr Roye 18	Mr Coxall 18
4	Mrs McArthur 24	Lady Donald 24
	Mr Huyjet 20	Mr Hitchcock 36

Result	*Gross*	*Hdc*	*Net*	
Mrs Harvey & Mr Hitchcock	100	19½	80½	
Miss Hale & Mr Berry	91	6	85	
Mrs McArthur & Mr Huyjet	107	22	85	
Mrs Hutton & Mr Watson	101	15	86	
Lady Donald & Mr Hitchcock	117	30	87	
Mrs Hutchinson & Mr Child	108	18½	89½	
Mrs Handon & Mr Coxall	109	18	91	
Miss Finch & Mr Newton	108	16	92	

The Artisan Members very kindly presented the winning lady with a box of chocolates.
The Beaconsfield Ladies presented the winning man with a box of cigarettes.

Result sheet of the first recorded ladies and artisans mixed foursomes competition in 1928

is, for example, the Preston Salver which was presented in 1935 by Mrs. J. Preston, but which together with the Wellesley-Colley Cup, was stolen from a member's house on 18th December 1953. The two trophies that are played for today are therefore not the original ones but the replacement trophies that the Ladies' section asked to be purchased with the insurance money.

The Raffety Vase is of particular interest because of its historical connotations. It was presented at the 1961 AGM of the Ladies' section by Mrs. Raffety, the wife of Vesey Raffety. In presenting the trophy, she said that she was doing so in memory of her father–in-law, Harold Raffety, who had been a member of the old Wilton Park Club, and also to mark the continuous association of the "Raffety" family name with the Club for more than fifty years.

The two most recent additions to the current list of named trophies are the Millennium Trophy and the Centenary Trophy, both purchased from contributions made by members of the Ladies' section. The former is a thirty-six hole medal competition while the latter, which will be awarded for the first time in the Club's centenary year, is awarded on the basis of points gained for placings in competitions throughout the year. Although new, these particular trophies will obviously find a place in the history of the Club.

The ladies at Beaconsfield have continued to play competitions in twoballs whereas the men changed to playing in threeballs several years ago. When in the 1980s the ladies requested an extension of their 1st tee reserved times on a Thursday, the Green Committee recommended to the Board that the ladies should play in threeballs, on the basis that, by doing so, no extension of time would be required. The secretary sought the advice of the LGU about this suggestion and was told that, as far as the Union was concerned, it was a matter entirely for the Ladies' Committee of each club to decide on the method of play, but the LGU added that "several Ladies' sections do now play in threes". Nevertheless, on the basis that the speed at which twoballs play would more than compensate for the fewer starting times, the ladies decided to retain the twoball tradition.

The Ladies Challenge Cup

The Ladies Club Championship was instituted as recently as 1951 but, for whatever reason, it was not played for after 1957 until it was "re-introduced" in 1974 when it was won by Mrs. Ann Laughland.

Since its re-introduction, the Ladies champion has been presented with the Bolton Cup, which is engraved with the words:

BEACONSFIELD GOLF CLUB

Ladies Challenge Cup

presented by

W. Ernest Bolton

The curious thing about this cup is that no-one seems to know where it came from or who Mr. Ernest Bolton may have been. Certainly the cup had a history long before it became the Ladies Challenge Cup because there are six shields on the cup indicating the names of the various ladies who won it (whether for golf or for some other sport is not stated) between 1902 and 1907. A Mrs. Eveline Clay won it in the last three of those six years and, since there are no other names on the cup until 1974, it is probably fair to assume that she was allowed to keep it in 1907. Where the cup has been since then until its re-emergence in 1974 remains a mystery. It is tempting to speculate that the cup was played for in the days of the old Wilton Park Golf Club and that it passed as some family heirloom from Mrs. Clay to Mr. Bolton but sadly, apart from a coincidence of dates, no evidence has yet come to light to support such speculation.

The names of the holders of the Ladies Challenge Cup are listed in Appendix 2 and it is somewhat remarkable that, over the last twenty-eight

Christine Watson receives the Bolton Cup from Judy Gill, the ladies captain, on winning the ladies club championship in the centenary year

years, only five different names have appeared on the Lady Champion Honours Board. It is equally remarkable that only one player should have won it in the last sixteen years – but then Christine Watson is a remarkable player.

Inter-Club Matches

The first recorded inter-club match was played at home against Denham on 12th May 1921. While it is pleasing to note from the match result sheet that Mrs. Hawley playing for Beaconsfield won by 5 and 4, the historian may perhaps be forgiven for not recording the result of the other seven matches.

Other early club matches included those against Harewood Downs in June 1922, which Beaconsfield won by 4½ matches to 3½ at home, against Ellesborough in May 1923, which was lost by 4 matches to 3 away and against West Middlesex at home in May 1924, when Beaconsfield won the singles by 6 matches to 2 and the foursomes by 3 matches to 1.

The team spirit was obviously a very strong element even in those days, so much so that in 1929 the Ladies' Committee decided that the Ladies' section should have a team tie in the colours of the Bucks County. The tie, which consisted of "a wide blue stripe, a wide red stripe with a very fine yellow stripe between them", could only be purchased and worn by members of one or

The ladies captain, Mrs. Brindle (3 handicap) driving from the 6th in 1932. She and Mrs. Tatham (7 handicap) were the first pair to represent Beaconsfield in the Ladies London Foursomes

other of the ladies' teams; for this purpose, a team member was defined as someone who had played in at least five matches in the same year.

Inter-club matches developed considerably over the years so that, by the time of the Second World War, the ladies had first or second team fixtures against eleven other clubs, including Ashridge, Burnham Beeches, Maidenhead, Moor Park, Stoke Poges, Temple and Wentworth. In addition, for many years there had been one match and frequently two matches each year against the artisans as well as mixed foursomes competitions with them. By 1953, one of these annual fixtures had been changed from a match into an annual mixed foursomes stableford competition in which each pairing comprised a lady member and an artisan and eventually that competition format (either as foursomes or greensomes) became the format for both the annual fixtures with the Artisans Club.

The Beaconsfield Salvers

The Beaconsfield Salvers thirty-six hole scratch medal foursomes competition has for some time been one of the leading amateur events for ladies in the south of England and its origin goes back to the annual Ladies Open Spring Meetings of the 1920s, the first and somewhat oblique reference to which is in a minute of the meeting of the Club's Committee held on 4th April 1924. The minute says nothing about the competition itself, but does address the serious problems that had been caused on the day of that particular competition due to the caddie-master having been an hour late for work; Colonel Du Pre undertook "to warn him that if it happened again, a change would need to be made". There is no record of the format of this Open Meeting at that time, but certainly by 1929 it consisted of an eighteen hole singles medal round in the morning followed after lunch by an eighteen hole foursomes bogey competition and it continued in that format until the outbreak of the Second World War.

There are no records as to when this Open Meeting was resumed after the war, but by 1955 it had come to be called the Beaconsfield Ladies Thirty-six Hole Open Medal Foursomes and it was a very prestigious event, as is reflected in the calibre of the winners of the salvers that year. They were Jacqueline Gordon, a Curtis Cup player in 1948, and Angela Ward, who went on to win the British Girls Championship when it was played at Beaconsfield later that same year. The following year, 1956, Angela played in the first of her six Curtis Cup matches. She married Michael Bonallack, the former secretary of the R&A and their daughter, Glenna Beasley, is now a regular competitor in the Beaconsfield Salvers.

As an aside, it should be mentioned that Beaconsfield members had a special interest in that 1955 British Girls Championship, not only because it was played at Beaconsfield, but also because one of their own junior members, Dolores Winsor, was playing in it. She was in fact beaten by Angela Ward, the eventual winner. Dolores had played in her first Girls Championship when it had been held at Beaconsfield in 1949 and had been runner-up in 1954. She was selected to play for Middlesex in 1955 and was runner-up in the DAKS Ladies Tournament the same year. In 1958 Dolores and Joyce Braddon were nominated to represent Beaconsfield in the Ladies London Foursomes and they reached the final.

The Beaconsfield Ladies Thirty-six Hole Open Medal Foursomes had thus resumed its place among the prestigious amateur ladies golfing events and its status was confirmed the following year, 1956, when it was won by the incomparable foursomes pairing of Zara Bolton, the Curtis Cup player and four times Curtis Cup Captain, and Elizabeth Price, who played in six Curtis Cup matches from 1950 to 1960.

Surprisingly, having attained such a status, the event was not held in 1957 because, so it is recorded, "petrol was still rationed". When it was resumed, it struggled to maintain its status and entries began to decline. Although various changes were tried, such as raising the handicap limits and making it a bogey rather than a medal competition, they were not successful and, at a meeting of the Ladies' Committee in November 1965, Joyce Braddon was moved to suggest that the salvers should be put away for a while and that, instead of the salvers, the winners should receive prizes. This appears to have been agreed for at a Ladies' Committee meeting three years later there was another discussion as to the future of "the two salvers that used to be played for in the thirty-six hole medal Open Foursomes." The "re-introduction of the Open Foursome Salver as before" was discussed on several subsequent occasions, but it was not until 1979 that the thirty-six hole medal foursomes was restored to the fixture list as "The Beaconsfield Ladies Open". Even so the salvers were not presented to the winners until 1996 by which time the quality of the entrants had so improved as to give proper prestige to the event. Since that time, all the winners of the "Beaconsfield Salvers" have had handicaps under 5.

One of the Beaconsfield salvers

The Ladies' Standard Scratch Score

Whatever may have been the position when the course opened in 1914, the first reference to the ladies' Standard Scratch Score is in connection with their first Autumn Meeting in October 1920 when the SSS was 81. Earlier that year the Ladies' Committee had invited Mrs. Newcombe from the LGU to visit the course "with a view to altering the ladies par for the course" but it is unclear whether she had been to the course by the time of the Autumn Meeting. However, two years later the LGU formally advised the Ladies' section that as from 1st January 1923 the SSS would be reduced from 79 to 78. This was because the 2nd hole was to be a bogey (par) 4 instead of 5.

Thereafter the ladies' SSS fluctuated up and down as, for example, when following the measurement of the ladies' course by tape in 1953, the SSS became 73 and then the introduction of a new tee at the 13th the very next year caused it to return to 74.

The location of ladies' tee at the 8th hole caused much discussion in the Ladies' Committee throughout the 1960s. The men's medal tee had already been moved from behind the 7th green to its present position to the left of that green but opinion was divided among the ladies as to whether their medal tee should be moved from the right to the left of the copse at the back of the 7th green – and in this discussion the effect that such a change would have on the SSS was much in evidence. In fact, over the next several years, the tee was moved several times between the two positions, but it has now been to the left of the copse for many years.

By 1970, the SSS had been reduced by the LGU to 73, but in the following year the LGU re-assessed the course at 74 because the 3rd hole had been lengthened by ten yards and a new tee at the 15th had lengthened that hole by thirty yards. The most recent assessment of the course in 1996 led to the SSS becoming 73 and so the 6th hole became a par 4.

The Ladies Stage Golfing Society

One of the earliest and leading ladies' golfing societies in the London area was the Ladies Stage Golfing Society which held its inaugural meeting at Beaconsfield in February 1921. Following this, the Society became affiliated to the Club which meant that, in return for an the agreed annual fee, individual members of the Society could play on the course at weekdays without charge, but at weekends and on public holidays a green fee was payable.

The Society, whose members have included such actresses as Felicity and Viola Beerbohm Tree, Gladys Cooper, Madge Saunders[†] and Mrs. Du Maurier, held its meetings at Beaconsfield for many years and their trophy for the best aggregate scratch score at the Spring and Autumn Meetings is still the Beaconsfield Challenge Bowl. The Society later moved to Addington where nearly all its records were destroyed by a fire just before the outbreak of war. In 1969, the Society was revived and celebrated its re-incarnation with a Spring Meeting at Beaconsfield on 22nd April. Joan Elliot, a founder member of the revived Society, was a member at Beaconsfield at the time and over the years several lady members of the Club have been and still are members of this Society. The Society still flourishes and now holds its meetings at Sunningdale Ladies Golf Club whose centenary also occurs in 2002 and whose course, like that at Beaconsfield, was designed by Harry Colt.

Achievements and Representative Honours

From the very early years of the Club, the Ladies' section has entered teams in various competitions in the county and the London area and has achieved a good measure of success. In 1922, Mrs. Brindle and Mrs. Tatham were the first pair to represent Beaconsfield in the prestigious Ladies London Foursomes. Since then the Club has frequently entered a team in this event but unfortunately has only managed to win it once; that was in 1954 when June Baucher and Joyce Braddon represented the Club. Four years later, Dolores Winsor and Joyce Braddon reached the final.

[†]Madge Saunders was the wife of Leslie Henson, the comedian who had caused Colonel Du Pre to lose his match against the Stage Golfing Society in 1920 by making him laugh so much.

Joan Elliot (ladies captain) holds the Bucks Challenge Shield flanked by her winning team in 1980
Left to right: Wendy Gardiner, Gill Goslett, Linda Wheater, Joan Elliot (ladies captain), Mary Bartlett,
Judy Warren, Ann Lauchland and Marian Rigby

The Bucks Challenge Shield was first played at Denham in 1927 when nine clubs in the county took part. Each club entered four players for the eighteen hole medal competition with the aggregate of the two best net scores counting. Beaconsfield won the Shield under this original format in 1931. In 1933, the format of the event was changed to a seven-a-side inter-club matchplay competition and Beaconsfield was the first winner in 1934 under the new format. It has subsequently won the Shield ten times.

It is always difficult to single out individuals from different eras for specific mention but, by common consent and with due apologies to others who are not included, the following lady members can be mentioned as having brought distinction to the Club through their golfing achievements:

PATIENCE WHITWORTH-JONES
buckinghamshire Ladies County champion in 1948 and 1949.

JUNE BAUCHER
Played for Buckinghamshire Ladies between 1954 and 1974, was Ladies County captain in 1955 and 1956 and Ladies County champion in 1956, 1957, 1962, 1963 and 1970. She was reserve for the English Ladies team in 1956. Playing for Beaconsfield, she and Joyce Braddon won the London Ladies Foursomes in 1954 and reached the final in 1955 and 1960.

Margaret Price – a member of the club since 1939

Christine Watson who has now won the ladies club championship for sixteen consecutive years

JOYCE BRADDON

Joyce joined Beaconsfield in 1948, was Buckinghamshire County captain in 1951, 1952 and 1965 and County president from 1983 to 1985. Joyce was Ladies County champion in 1952 and together with June Baucher won the London Ladies Foursomes in 1954 and reached the finals in 1955 and 1960.

KATHY COPLEY

Buckinghamshire County champion in 1980, a Scottish International in 1974 and 1975. Runner-up in the Scottish Ladies championship in 1969 and 1974.

NANCYE GOLD

Nancye was a member of the Club before it became a members' Club and was one of the two lady members of the Board of Directors when it became a members' Club. She was County captain in 1927 and 1932 and County champion nine times in the period from 1928 to 1951.

MARGARET (GREAVES) PRICE

Joined Beaconsfield in 1939, was captain in 1948 and 1962 and in 1989 she was made a Life Member of the Club to mark her many contributions to the Club over her fifty years of membership.

Margaret is now well over ninety but is still a member after more than sixty years. In 1956, she married Ivor Price, a member and former captain of the club. She was a member of the British Ladies Open Championship Committee in 1955, captain of the English Ladies team in the Home Internationals in 1956 and captain of the English Girls Team who played their championships at Beaconsfield in 1948, 1949, 1955 and 1961.

JUDY WARREN

Judy was Buckinghamshire Ladies County champion in 1981, 1982 and 1984.

CHRISTINE WATSON

Christine, prior to joining Beaconsfield in 1987, had been an England Girl International in 1969 and 1970, had played for the English Ladies team in 1982 and was a finalist in the English Ladies' championship in 1982. Having been Middlesex County champion for four years in the early 1980s, she became Buckinghamshire County champion in 1987, the year she joined Beaconsfield and, in the ensuing fifteen years, has only failed to win that title on three occasions. Christine was an England selector from 1992 to 1995, and has won numerous scratch competitions in the south of England as well as the Ladies' Club Championship continuously since 1986. She holds the ladies' course record (69) at Beaconsfield, Pinner Hill and Hendon. Christine was Buckinghamshire County captain for 1998-2000, and was appointed an ELGA SSS assessor for ten years from 1996. She was elected to the Board of the Club in 1996 and was made a Life Member in 2000.

With the number of junior girl members that the Club now has and with the commitment and enthusiasm of the Junior Golf's organisers, there is every prospect that these achievements and representative honours will continue.

Chapter Thirteen

The Juniors, the Wildebeests and the Seniors

The Juniors

PARTLY BECAUSE of its image as an old man's game, partly because it was not regarded as a team game and partly because of the lack of access to courses, junior golf was not a significant feature of sporting life between the wars. Clubs such as Beaconsfield did permit juniors to become members, but such membership was for the most part restricted to sons and daughters of members and in most Clubs junior members were not permitted to use the course at weekends. Not surprisingly, therefore, there are few mentions of junior members in the Club's earliest surviving records and none at all about junior competitions and matches.

The need to encourage young people to become members of the Club was recognised after the war by Colonel Du Pre himself who, as mentioned in a previous chapter, initiated a new category of Intermediate Full Membership. And when the Club became a members' Club in 1948, this new category of membership not only ceased to be restricted to sons and daughters of members but its upper age limit was raised to thirty. Moreover, within that category, the subscription started at two guineas and increased by stages (albeit unequally as between males and females) until, at the upper age limit, it was still one guinea below that for Five-day membership.

The first active steps taken by the members' Club to encourage junior golf were largely initiated by members of the Ladies' section. Florence Duncan, the first elected woman director of the members Club, reported at the December 1949 Board meeting that, in the first year since becoming a members' Club, the number of junior boys had increased from eight to fourteen while that for junior girls had dropped from four to two. She went on to announce a new initiative whereby two members, a Mrs. Handford and Margaret Greaves (then captain of the English Girls Team and to whom reference was made in the previous chapter), had agreed to set up and take charge of "children's classes" and that Alex Crombie, the Club professional, would be very much involved. There was to be a one hour class on a Tuesday

152

morning, "or on a Friday if wet", during the school holidays and a charge of 7s.6d. was to be made for the four weekly lessons. Those taking part would be expected to bring their own "iron clubs" and the professional would lend them putters and balls. The scheme was open to the children of non-members as well as those of members although, in the former case, their parents would be asked to pay an extra "club fee" of 2s.6d. per lesson. Some forty-eight children joined the classes the following Easter, but as is so often the case with well intentioned initiatives, it was not possible to maintain such high numbers all the time and the numbers attending these holiday classes fluctuated considerably over subsequent years.

In 1958, Lindsay Robertson, a director and former captain, presented a cup for a Stableford competition to be arranged for the junior members and the first winner was Peter Ellis. Since only seven juniors participated, it was decided that in future the competition should be played, as it is now, during the Easter holidays when more juniors would be available rather than in September. When the trophy was played for during the next Easter vacation, a member who wished to be identified only as "Autolycus" generously presented two dozen golf balls for prizes. The Robertson Trophy was won that year and again the following year (1960) by Andrew Davidson whose father and mother, Bill and Margot Davidson, had the unique distinction in 1964 of being captain and Ladies' captain in the same year. In the 1960 competition, Chris Plumridge returned a net 64 playing off a 7 handicap – and with such a score he understandably still feels somewhat peeved at only being runner-up.

This junior golf initiative became somewhat more formalised in 1959 when the captain, Douglas Gordon,[†] declared his full support for the development of junior golf, charged the Green Committee with responsibility for continuing it and asked his vice-captain, Lt. Colonel Taylor, to assume a personal responsibility. A notice in the Club dated 24th December 1959 indicates the enthusiasm that had been engendered in the Juniors section at that time read:

> The number of Junior members who turned up for the course of lessons on the first day was more than twice the number expected. This was a very gratifying result of the efforts being made to help the Juniors, but it was found impossible to cope with such large numbers in an afternoon. Instead of twice a week therefore, the professional will now set apart four afternoons a week for these lessons.

The notice went on to divide the juniors into four groups for future lessons which were to start on 29th December. Ken Rumens, Paul Godfrey, Patricia Mawhood, Linda and Hillary Edwards and Martin Rumens are but a few of the names mentioned.

†On his retirement as captain, Douglas donated the set of galvanised posts and chains that still surround the back and sides of the 1st tee.

Beaconsfield Girls Juniors in 2000
Back row left to right: Lucy Joyce, Hayly Christian, Hilda Wright (Junior Girls organiser),
Christine Watson, Gemma Byrne, Alex Fee, Candice Miles.
Front row left to right: Lisa Rowles, Amy Duncan, Anna Jones, Victoria Carroll,
Victoria Harris, Rachel Drummond, Jennifer McSloy

From time to time, other members have taken on the challenge of organising junior classes, competitions and matches and some current members will still recall the years from the mid-1970s when Ken Braddon, a scratch golfer for many years and the first Club champion, was the junior golf organiser. His own son, Richard, had been a junior member of the Club and had won the British Boys Championship at Moortown in 1958. Not surprisingly Ken was a very enthusiastic organiser of the juniors who prospered under his encouraging, if somewhat demanding, approach to the task. The practice of allowing promising junior members to play in adult competitions under certain conditions was initiated by Ken Braddon though not without much opposition at the time.

The last twenty years or so have been a very successful period for junior golf at the Club, due in large measure to the commitment and enthusiasm of Junior Golf organisers such as George Irving, John Edwards, Colin Biffa and Walter Gutteridge and their several assistants, and to the coaching provided by the Club's professionals. Without doubt, the two most accomplished golfers to have come through the junior ranks in recent years are Freddie George and Luke Donald whose achievements are mentioned in other

Luke Donald

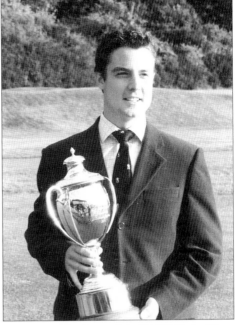

Peter Neal, winner of the BB&O Under 21 Championship in 2001

chapters,† but several other junior boys, such as Peter Neal, Andrew Codling, Robert Christian, Stephen Farr and Ben Scevity, have all had achievements beyond the Club's competitions and have all been called upon to represent the county at various age levels.

As regards the junior girls, special mention must be made of Hilda Wright, a member of the Ladies' section. In 1997, the county was struggling to find just seven girls who had handicaps and who could therefore play in county matches. Hilda recognised the challenge and, through initial golf classes at the school where she teaches, Hilda has been able to bring several girls to junior membership of the Club and this has led to other girls joining, so that now there are twenty-one junior girl members of the Club – the envy of many other clubs in the county and elsewhere. Three of these girls, Hayley Christian, Vicky Hamilton and Liza Rowles, already play in the County Girls team. Hilda's knowledge and experience of junior girls' golf has enabled her to write a series of booklets that explain the game of golf, its rules and etiquette, in a simplified and interesting way; *Emily Tees Off* and *Emily Plays From Tee To Green* have already been published and a third booklet is being prepared.

†Freddie George in Chapter Eleven and Luke Donald in Chapter Fourteen.

Emily tees off

Junior team successes in recent years have included winning the Chiltern Junior League in 1998 and, in the same year, qualifying at the Vale Golf and Country Club for the national semi-finals of the SAAB – Daily Mail Junior Inter-Club Competition at Stoke Park. The team that qualified in that event – Andrew Codling, Peter Neal, Stephen Farr, Richard Clarke, Robert Christian and Robert Greenfield, with Barry Cotter as travelling reserve – was probably the strongest junior team the Club has ever had. This centenary year the junior team has already qualified for the regional final of the British Heart Foundation Junior Golf Championship, which will be played at Gog Magog Golf Club.

The Wildebeests

Knowing that the wildebeest is a large African antelope with a head resembling that of an ox, a short mane, a beard and a tufted tail, new members (who may themselves one day become gnu members) as well as visitors to the Club are often curious when they see references on Club notice boards to the Beaconsfield Wildebeests. Speculation grows as to whether these creatures are derived from species at local zoos or whether they might have been brought back from deepest Africa by former colonial members.

If truth be told, the connection between the Beaconsfield Wildebeests and the equally noble creatures of South Africa is tenuous in the extreme for the evolution of the Beaconsfield species is much more recent and, indeed, much better documented than is that of its African counterpart, for it was only thirty years ago that it was first identified.

It was in 1972 that Richard Smedley-Wild, a member of Gerrards Cross and Stoke Poges as well as Beaconsfield, organised two friendly fourball better ball matches against Stoke Poges on a home and away basis for players with handicaps of 10 and higher. Both matches were won by the home side and by the same margin and these were the first two matches played by this newly discovered but, as yet, unnamed species. The golfing and social success of these two matches led to similar ones being arranged with Gerrards Cross the following year with equal success.

However, at that time, these matches were entirely unofficial, but by 1975 the number of members interested in playing in them had increased to such a level that more matches were required to satisfy the demand. Thus, an approach was made to the Club captain at that time, Derek Randall, to see if club matches for non-single figure handicap golfers could be incorporated into the Club's Fixture List. Permission was given but only on the basis that no extra work should fall on the Club's secretariat, which meant that the task of organising such matches had to be undertaken by interested and committed members. At first, it was Richard Smedley-Wild himself who

Beaconsfield Wildebeests and Henley Seniors competed for the Basil Evans Trophy in September 1998. Walter Gutteridge (Beaconsfield captain) and Rodney Lunn (Henley captain) are seen holding the Ryder Cup

shouldered that burden, but for the last seventeen years this task has been most efficiently and enthusiastically fulfilled by Reg Rundle – the much respected leader of the pack.

Since the successes of the early matches against Stoke Poges and Gerrards Cross, other clubs have been approached and today home and away matches are also played annually against Burnham Beeches, Henley, Moor Park and West Hill.

But whence "Wildebeests"? The name owes its origin to the fact that Moor Park had a more sophisticated handicapping classification than Beaconsfield and the other clubs so that when they were approached about playing one of these "friendly" fixtures, Beaconsfield was offered a choice of playing against their "Foxes" (players with handicaps of 10 to 18) or against their "Rabbits" (those with handicaps 19 to 24). Naturally, Beaconsfield chose the Foxes – but clearly a name worthy of the Beaconsfield combatants was needed. The Beaconsfield Wildebeests had arrived.

The Beaconsfield Wildebeest is well known for his modesty and shyness, but on the afternoon of 26th September 1998, several of them were actually caught on camera. At first sight, it might appear from the resulting photograph that they were playing in the Ryder Cup match for, indeed, it was the actual Ryder Cup that the two captains of the day, Walter Gutteridge of

157

Beaconsfield and Rodney Lunn of Henley, were caught holding. But, in reality, the occasion was a far more challenging one than that for it was the away leg against Henley of the annual match for the prestigious Basil Evans Cup. And the Ryder Cup? Well, it just happened to be on loan to the Henley Club at the time for a wholly unconnected purpose.

In 1993, Moor Park initiated an annual event called the "Foxes Festival" in which teams consisting of players from each of the (then) nine clubs involved competed on an "Am-Am" basis over eighteen holes. Most fittingly, Reg Rundle was a member of the winning team and his hole in one at the 10th on the High Course was not his only contribution. This event proved to be very popular and is now hosted each year by one or other of the clubs involved. It so happened that Beaconsfield played host to the Foxes Festival in May 2002 its centenary year, and it is pleasing to record that a Beaconsfield member, Tom Webb, was one of the winning team.

Richard Smedley-Wild would, indeed, be overjoyed that his idea of using the underplayed Sunday afternoons at Beaconsfield for a social contact with fellow golfers from neighbouring clubs has endured for so long. It remains the policy of the Wildebeests to give all players who indicate their interest a chance to play but, on some occasions in recent times, it has been difficult to field a team. It is to be hoped that the Beaconsfield Wildebeest is not becoming an endangered species

Seniors Golf

There are no records to indicate that, prior to its becoming a members' Club in 1948, there was any differentiation among members of the Club on the grounds of age. The 1939 Fixture List, for example, contains no reference to competitions or matches for Seniors.

In fact, the first reference to a playing age differentiation comes in February 1956 when the Board decided that, in order to encourage "older male members" to play in Club competitions, those over seventy who wished to do so (and who were prepared to bear the slings and arrows of outraged colleagues) could play off the ladies' tees. However, such a concession was thought by some members to have been overly generous for, in 1960, the Green Committee discussed for some time a suggestion that the handicap of those competitors who did take advantage of the concession should be reduced by four strokes for the purposes of any competition in which they played. In the event, the Green Committee could not reach agreement on the matter and the suggestion was dropped – at least until the following year when the captain, Charles Crockwell, raised it again. In his view, the handicaps of members over seventy were too low when they were playing on other courses and he suggested that all their handicaps should be raised by four strokes with the one exception that, if they chose to play off the ladies' tees in competitions at Beaconsfield, they should forfeit those four strokes. The Green Committee considered this proposal most carefully, emanating as it did from the captain, but found itself unable to agree. In any case, the whole matter was finally brought to an end in 1962 when the Board itself cancelled altogether the concession that male members over seventy could play off the ladies' tees.

In putting his thoughts together some years ago about the origins of "Seniors' Golf" at Beaconsfield, the late Hamish Wilson referred to this group of members, of whom of course he was one, as the "Twilight Brigade". However apt that description may have been at the time of his writing, more than a decade of early retirements have lately brought the brigade to something more akin to Divisional strength – or so it would seem to

Hamish Wilson, 1980

some of the other members. Moreover, many of them are still recognisable as virile Wildebeest material.

The Seniors Roll-ups

According to Hamish, the Friday morning and the Tuesday afternoon roll-ups started in the early 1970s as "two separate factions". The Friday morning phenomenon started as a single fourball comprising Ken Gillett, Doug Day, Jimmy Rellie and Joe White but, as the numbers turning up began to grow, it became inevitable that there had to be a draw. Initially, these Friday morning draws were organised by Ken Gillett promptly at 8.45 a.m. and it was Ken apparently who produced the old cigar box containing slithers of cardboard on which the names of the players were written as and when they arrived. At the appointed hour, the pack was shuffled and drawn in fours for the pairings and for the order of play. This informal Friday roll-up still takes place throughout the year, but on the last Friday in the months from April to September the 1st tee is reserved from 8.15 a.m. to 8.45 a.m. when a Stableford competition with an entry fee of fifty pence is played. There is no organiser for the roll-up except for the competition days.

The Tuesday afternoon faction, as Hamish termed it, started out initially as two fourballs, one comprising Arnold Lewis, Jimmy Adair, Jimmy Rellie, and Bob Lawes and the other comprising Tom Brown, Martin Hebb, Arthur

Nicholls and Joe White. Again, numbers turning up grew quite quickly so that eventually a draw became necessary. The procedure was much the same then as it is now in that those wanting to play assembled in the Men's Bar (as it then was) and at the appropriate time the draw for pairings and for the order of play was made by selecting a numbered card from the pack. Gerry Fenner has been the efficient and most enthusiastic organiser of this roll-up for the past twelve years or so.

Seniors Inter-club Matches

Although an informal seniors match against the Denham seniors was arranged in 1968, it was not really until Tom Brown's initiatives in the mid-1970s that such matches really began to become established in the Club's Fixture List. The first fixture that Tom arranged was against Harpenden, closely followed by ones with Stoke Poges, Berkhamsted, Ellesborough and Burnham Beeches. Matches against Ashridge, Harewood Downs, Frilford Heath, Woburn and Temple came to be added later.

Some of the teams competing in these inter-club matches have adopted names such as the Ellesborough "Elders", the Harpenden "Drones" and "The Lays" of Burnham Beeches – whose captain is known as "The Warden". The Beaconsfield team has been known from the outset by the somewhat negative name of "Beaconsfield Bogeys" – said to have been suggested by Tommy Brown.

Annual home and away matches against The Oxfordshire were added to the Fixture List in 1997. The trophy for which the matches are played was kindly donated by The Oxfordshire; it contains a holder for a golf ball and the rules of the trophy command that a ball bearing the logo of the losing team be "ceremonially but without triumphalism" placed in that holder at the presentation and remain there until the presentation the following year.

The long-standing connection between seniors of Beaconsfield and L'Association de Seniors de Golf de Belgique (ASGB) began in 1953 when one of the Beaconsfield members, Jack Bracey-Gibbon – a senior executive with the Belgian company, Agfa-Geveart – received Board approval for a team of seniors to play a match against what was described as a "Belgian Touring Team" composed primarily of members of the Royal Antwerp Golf Club. The first match was played at Beaconsfield on 21st June 1953 and, though not official club fixtures, subsequent home and away matches have been played although not every year. Away matches have been noted for the splendour of the hospitality that has been extended by the hosts. After Jack's death in 1973, Harold Staines and Alan Neale were the prime organisers of these matches against the Belgian seniors but, since the formation of the Seniors' Committee in the early 1990s, that task now falls to the secretary of the

Seniors' section. The most recent of these matches was played at the Royal Antwerp Golf Club in September 2000 and designated the "Millenium Match". The enjoyment of the match by both sides was such that it is really unnecessary to record that the away team lost by 20 points to 10.

Seniors and Veterans Competitions

Enjoyable as the inter-club matches are, the three annual eighteen hole Stableford competitions are probably the highlights of the seniors' year.

The Spring Meeting was first held in 1994 and the trophy for this competition is now a silver fruit bowl presented in 2001 by Jock Moffat, a long-standing member of the Club. This bowl was originally presented by Jock on his retirement from the army to the Headquarters Mess of the Royal Army Educational Corps for use on regimental dinner nights. However, when in 1992 the RAEC lost its individual identity and its HQ Officers Mess, such pieces of donated silver were returned to their respective benefactors. The generous donation of this bowl to the Club by a former member of the Corps forges yet another link between the Club and the RAEC.

The Seniors Invitation Meeting held each May is followed in the autumn by the competition for the Beaconsfield Bowl, now usually referred to as the "Bogeys Bowl", which was donated in 1982 by Colin Paterson.

In addition to these stableford competitions, there is the singles match play competition for the Senior Golfers Cup presented in 1952 and the keenly contested Seniors Winter League. Since 1979, at the instigation of Joan Mawhood when she was Ladies' captain, the seniors have had a mixed competition each year with the Ladies' section.

And for those seniors whose golfing life continues, or even begins, at the age of sixty-five, the Veteran Golfers Cup, presented in 1984, and the Pensioners Putting Pot presented in 1991 by Ken Johnson, are additional knock-out competitions.

The Seniors Committee

For a long time after it had become a members' Club, such organisation as there was for seniors golf came from the enthusiasm and commitment of individual members and, in the more recent years, no one was more committed and involved than Hamish Wilson himself. It was altogether most fitting that, in 1991, he was made a Life Member of the Club "especially having regard to his running of the seniors section for many years". The Seniors' section has never been a club within a club, but for the last decade or so the considerable expansion of its activities has led to its having its own committee consisting of the section's chairman, its treasurer and its very hardworking secretary.

Chapter Fourteen

Honorary Membership

ALTHOUGH THERE do not appear to have been any Honorary Members of the Wilton Park Club, Colonel Du Pre's commitment to making the new Beaconsfield Club one of the prestigious ones in the London area is well reflected in the invitations that were made in the early years to distinguished people, especially in the worlds of golf and politics, to become Honorary Members of the Club.

The first Honorary Member appears to have been Mr. C. Humphrey Roberts who was given the honour in August 1919 on his resignation as temporary secretary of the Club. Mr. Roberts, who was probably a member of the Club, acted as secretary of the Club (and of the company) while the permanent secretary, Major F. Pellew, was away on military service during the First World War.

In remarkable contrast to the somewhat parochial nature of the first Honorary Membership, the Committee's second recorded venture into this particular area only some seven months later was at an altogether different level. A minute of the Committee meeting held on 6th March 1920, reads very simply and succinctly as follows: "It was decided to ask H.R.H. The Prince of Wales to become an Honorary Member. Secretary to arrange."

Unfortunately, there is no further information as to what, if anything, happened to that particular initiative and since there is no further reference to this matter in the records, it must be assumed that it was not progressed or that the invitation was graciously declined. Perhaps it is significant that Colonel Du Pre himself was not at the Committee meeting at which the decision had been taken.

Altogether more successful, so it would appear, was the Committee's resolution in the following March (1921) to invite Mr. Lloyd George, then Liberal Prime Minister of the coalition government, to become an Honorary Member. This time the minute included the words: "Colonel Du Pre to undertake the necessary steps."

Colonel Du Pre was still Conservative MP for South Bucks at the time, and obviously had the appropriate political connections, and while there is no actual record of Colonel Du Pre's steps having been successful, they clearly were because, alas, two years later, in May 1923, the Committee resolved that the name of Lloyd George be "removed from the list" of Honorary Members. Perhaps understandably, no explanation is given in the Minutes.

Whether or not it was so initially is not known, but the receiving of Honorary Membership at Beaconsfield Golf Club was, or at least became, something of a fragile blessing, for it was not granted for life or even for as long as the recipients behaved themselves. It was granted, as one might say of short tenancies, for one year only renewable annually. Indeed, by 1922 an annual review of Honorary Memberships seems to have become so much the established practice that, at a Committee meeting held on 4th March that year, it was formalised in a resolution requiring that "… the list of Honorary Members be brought before the first Committee after 1st June each year for revision."

A minute of this same meeting in March 1922 records, somewhat peremptorily and again without explanation, that "the following names be removed from the list":

> Rt. Reverend the Bishop of Buckingham
> Rt. Hon. Lord Foster
> G. L. Taylor

Why the first two were removed is not known, but the G. L. Taylor to whom reference is made was George Langley-Taylor who was Colonel Du Pre's land agent at Wilton Park. He had been made an Honorary Member while he was acting as interim secretary of the Club and was removed from the list in 1922 when Major Sarel was appointed secretary. The practice, which became a tradition, of making the secretary of the Club an Honorary Member stems from these early days.

It was also at this same March meeting that four of the best amateur golfers of the time were invited to become Honorary Members:

Reymond H. de Montmorency	Roger H. Wethered
Bernard Darwin	Cyril J. H. Tolley

Letters appreciating and accepting the honour were duly received from each of these golfers the following month.

The appointment of these four golfers affords considerable insight into the high standing and good contacts that Beaconsfield Golf Club was developing in the golfing world so soon after its inception. Veteran golfers of today may not need to be reminded of the achievements of these legends who dominated amateur golf between the wars, but a brief account of their standing in the world of golf may help younger members and posterity to appreciate how much the association of the names of such players with club added to its stature.

The first Walker Cup match was played in the U.S.A. on 29th August 1922 at the Long Island Golf Club, New York, when the American team won by 8 matches to 4. However, what is generally regarded as the historical origin of the Walker Cup series was the unofficial match played the year before on 21st May 1921, at the Royal Liverpool Golf Club at Hoylake between a team of leading British amateur golfers and a team from the U.S.A. – which, sad to say, the U.S.A. won by 9 matches to 3. All four players who were invited to become Honorary Members at Beaconsfield had been members of that British team the previous year (Ireland was included in the following year) and all but de Montmorency played in the first Walker Cup match in 1922. In fact, Roger Wethered and Cyril Tolley went on to play in several Walker Cup matches after that.

REYMOND HERVEY DE MONTMORENCY

Reymond Hervey de Montmorency was a distinguished amateur golfer at the international level who, at the peak of his career, played off a handicap of plus 4. In 1935, he became President of the English Golf Union.

De Montmorency was also a dominant and respected figure in the local area of Buckinghamshire and Berkshire. Professionally, he was a languages master at Eton College from 1900 to 1926 and he became a housemaster there. Fortunately, his professional career left him time enough to pursue not only his amateur career as an international golfer but also as a dedicated local club golfer (and no mean cricketer either). He was a member of

Burnham Beeches Golf Club (where he was captain in 1903), a member of Datchet Golf Club (where he was President from 1921 to 1929) and he was very much involved with Stoke Poges Golf Club (as it then was) and his name appears several times on its honours board.

De Montmorency was a member at Beaconsfield before becoming an Honorary Member and had captained the men's team that played against the prestigious Lady Golfers Club at Beaconsfield in 1921. Unlike that of some others, his Honorary Membership was continued until his death in 1938. His daughter, Ann, an acknowledged pianist and painter as well as a very well known lady golfer, was married to the the *Daily Telegraph*'s celebrated cricket and rugby correspondent, E. W. "Jim" Swanton, for forty years and died his widow in November 1998. An extensive obituary including a photograph of Ann with her father appeared in The Times.

Roger Wethered

ROGER WETHERED

Roger Wethered was one of the outstanding amateur golfers in the period between the two world wars, playing in six Walker Cup matches from 1922 to 1934 and for England against Scotland in the eight years from 1922. In 1921, the year before he was made an Honorary Member of Beaconsfield Golf Club, he had tied with Jock Hutchison in the Open Championship, but lost in the play-off. He was captain of the R&A in 1946. Roger's sister, Joyce, (later Lady Heathcoat-Amery) was an equally famous amateur golfer who, in 1922, won the first of her four Ladies' British Open Amateur titles.

BERNARD DARWIN

Bernard Darwin is perhaps more famous for his writings, especially about golf, than he is for his skill at the game itself. Nevertheless, he was a very accomplished player who played for England in many International matches between 1902 and 1924. He was for many years Golf Correspondent of The Times and it was in that capacity that he had the remarkable distinction of going to America in 1922 to cover the first Walker Cup match for that newspaper and of ending up playing for and, indeed, captaining the Great Britain and Ireland side when the appointed captain became too ill to participate. He was captain of the R&A in 1934-1935.

Bernard Darwin

Cyril Tolley

Because of his standing and his graceful, yet authoritative, manner of writing, Bernard Darwin was frequently asked to write appreciations of golf clubs and their courses and, in 1925, he produced the one on *The Beaconsfield Golf Club* which is referred to in other chapters. It is interesting that, playing off plus 1, he played in the top single for Beaconsfield against the Lady Golfers Club in the annual match in 1925 when he beat Miss Helme (3 handicap) by 2 and 1 – despite her receiving 9 courtesy shots.

CYRIL TOLLEY

Cyril Tolley was another of the great amateurs of the 1920s and 1930s, but he was an altogether more dynamic and flamboyant character than his contemporaries. He also played in the first Walker Cup match in 1922 and in five further matches, being captain of the team in 1924. In 1930, Tolley met the great Bobby Jones in the fourth round of the British Amateur Championship at St Andrews – only to lose at the 19th when Jones laid him a stymie.

For a reason perhaps only known to the Committee of the day, while the Honorary Memberships of de Montmorency, Wethered and Darwin were renewed annually for several years, that of Cyril Tolley was not. In fact, his name does not even appear in the list of Honorary Members approved by the Committee only two years after he was appointed. Perhaps his flamboyant life-style was just too much for the Beaconsfield Golf Club of the day! That, however, did not see the end of Cyril Tolley at Beaconsfield for, in 1927, when the prestigious Golf Illustrated Gold Vase was played here, he was beaten by Roger Wethered in this 36 hole competition by just one stroke.

Later in that same year, July 1922, another very distinguished golfer, this time a lady golfer, who had many associations over the years with Beaconsfield Golf Club, was appointed an Honorary Member. She was Miss Cecil Leitch.

CECIL LEITCH

Miss Leitch was probably the most phenomenal lady golfer of her time – equalled in stature perhaps only by her great rival, Joyce Wethered. She won the French Ladies Championship five times between 1912 and 1924, the British Ladies Championship four times between 1914 and 1926 and (apart from the war years) she played for England in the Ladies Home Internationals from 1910 to 1928.

It is probable that Cecil Leitch was a member of the Club before she was made an Honorary Member. The previous year, she had been invited to become the Club's first Ladies' captain and that is unlikely to have happened if she was not already a member. Moreover, in 1921 she and a Mr. W. E. Broomfield had been the first winners of the

Wilton Park Challenge Bowl and theirs were the first names to be inscribed on the same trophy that is still played for each year. Be that as it may, the following year, 1922, Miss Leitch was appointed an Honorary Member of the Club – "for one year"!

Cecil Leitch at Beaconsfield

Over the following decade or so various dignitaries, including "the American Ambassador" (unnamed) in 1922 and Stanley Baldwin (then Conservative Prime Minister) in 1925, were added to and then often deleted from the list of Honorary Members the following year. The annual "renewability" of Honorary Membership made it something of a precarious privilege.

During the 1930s, the list of Honorary Members grew longer and longer until the list approved by the Committee in June 1938 "for the year ending 31st May 1939" contained no less than the following fourteen names:

De Montmorency.
Lord Desborough (known to have been President of the Club in 1922 and probably its first President).
Captain R. C. E. Herbert.
Bernard Darwin.
Charles Du Pre.
C. H. Roberts (the same person who had been the Club's acting secretary during the First World War).
Major W. G. M. Sarel (who had been secretary of the Club from 1922 to 1928 and a well-known Sussex cricketer).
M. G. Townley.
G. Langley-Taylor (Colonel Du Pre's agent).
Lady Churston.
Mrs. Herbert.
Mrs. Durham.
Miss Macfarlane.
Miss Bartier (then secretary of the Lady Golfers Club).

The Honorary Memberships of what may perhaps be called this "core" group continued to be renewed on a yearly basis, with the occasional addition and deletion, until the early 1950s by which time nature had

167

Richard Braddon, winner of the British Boys Championship held at Moortown, 1958

taken its toll of many of them. One of the additions to the list in 1950 was Miss Laidler who, it will be recalled, had leased Golf Lodge during the war and who was headmistress at the girls school on Longbottom Lane for many years. The pupils of that school had enjoyed a special playing rate at the Club of 30s. per term.

There was a rather curious, though entirely understandable, use of Honorary Membership in 1948. At its meeting on 10th January that year, the Committee decided to invite the secretaries of some forty of London's most prestigious gentlemen's clubs to become Honorary Members "for the period of the present petrol restrictions in order to give them the right to introduce their members at the 'member introduced' rates". The Clubs included The Athenaeum, Boodles, Brooks, The Carlton, The Junior Carlton, The Caledonian, Whites, The Army and Navy and so on. It was further agreed to enclose with each letter of invitation a note saying:

> The Committee of Beaconsfield Golf Club wish to advise your golfing members that its Club is of very easy access by train either from Marylebone or Paddington as the clubhouse is alongside Seer Green Halt which is between Gerrards Cross and Beaconsfield stations. During the present petrol restrictions, the Committee would like to offer your members and their families, on introduction from you, Temporary Membership.

The note went on to set out the reduced terms for differing periods of membership, the green fees and the price of meals (lunch at 5s. and afternoon tea at 1s.6d.). It also enclosed a copy of the current train timetable. There can be little doubt that this initiative was part of the drive to build up the membership of the Club after the war and as it was about to become a members' Club. It is most disappointing not to find any information as to how successful the initiative was.

At the Club's twentieth AGM in 1968, Charles Crockwell, who had been a member for many years and captain in 1961, was made an Honorary Member in recognition of his services to the Club in stepping into the post of secretary of the Club from 1963 to 1968.

Peter Alliss becomes an honorary member of the Club in 1998
Left to right: Ken Robertson (captain), Jackie Alliss, Mary Horgan (Ladies captain), Peter Alliss,
Gordon Tuck (immediate past captain) and Derek Randall (president)

From an early date it became the custom to make the secretary and the professional Honorary Members of the Club and this custom has frequently been extended to the vicars of Seer Green.

In 1958, Richard Braddon, the son of Ken and Joyce Braddon, was made an Honorary Member on the occasion of his winning the British Boys Championship – but only until he reached his majority. Not since then had anyone been made an Honorary Member of the Club on account of his or her outstanding contribution to the world of golf until, forty years later, two such people were invited within twelve months of each other to accept the privilege – namely, Peter Alliss and Luke Donald.

PETER ALLISS

Peter's achievements as a professional golfer – including the Spanish, Italian, Portuguese and Brazilian Opens, more than twenty other major tournaments, the highly prized Vardon Trophy in three successive years and no less than eight Ryder Cup matches between 1953 and 1964 – are well known. So also are his achievements as a prolific writer on golfing matters and as a radio and television commentator. It was on account of all these achievements coupled with his links to the Club through his father that the Board felt it appropriate to extend the honour to him, just as it had to his father in a somewhat different age. Peter received his Honorary Membership at a Dinner held in his honour at the clubhouse on 11th December 1998, and among the congratulatory messages that he received was one from Severiano Ballesteros which read:

Luke Donald, the first member of the Club to become a Walker Cup player, receives honorary membership from Allan Robertson, the captain. The Walker Cup was on display

… my heartfelt congratulations for being named Honorary Member of such a prestigious Club as Beaconsfield … Golf in the British Isles owes you so much as you have devoted most of your life to it. You mean everything to the game and this makes you admired and appreciated among all of us …

Among the many who have received Honorary Membership of the Club over the last hundred years, none has more thrilled the entire membership and none has been more worthy of the appointment than Luke Donald.

LUKE DONALD

Luke Donald first showed an interest in golf at the age of eight while on a family holiday in La Manga and when he applied to become a junior member at Beaconsfield in October 1991 at the age of fifteen he already had a handicap of 5. It was not long before his enormous potential began to appear for in the following year he became the first junior member to win the Club Championship as well as the Secretary's Putter. In 1994, he won the Montrose Cloete Cup and success in Club competitions quickly turned into success at County level and, by 1996, at International level when he played several times for the full England team.

Luke's considerable achievements as an amateur golfer and, at the age of twenty-four, as one of the world's top three amateurs, are recorded in Appendix 3. Suffice to say that his most notable achievements as an amateur were his selection for the Great Britain and Ireland Walker Cup teams to play the U.S.A. first at Nairn in September 1999, (when he secured maximum points in his singles and foursomes matches) and then at the Sea Island course, Ocean Forest, Georgia, in 2001. In those two Walker Cup matches, both of which were won by the Great Britain and Ireland team, Luke won seven out of his eight matches.

Some measure of Luke's stature in the world of amateur golf can be gathered from the letters of tribute that were read out on the occasion of the Club's function on Tuesday 14th December 1999, at which his Honorary Membership was conferred and at which Luke was presented with a specially commissioned painting of the clubhouse by Denis Pannett.

Michael Bonnallack (now Sir Michael) then captain of the R&A wrote:

In September last year, I was delighted to finish my term as secretary by being at Nairn for the Walker Cup victory and, again, seeing Luke play such magnificent golf. However, it is not only his skill on the golf course but it is also the way in which he conducts himself and especially his modesty which is so impressive.

Peter Alliss wrote:

It may surprise you to know that I've followed your career in the United States more closely than your golfing exploits in Europe … I can assure you, if you don't already know, you have taken the collegiate scene by storm and have achieved things that even Tiger Woods has not managed to do.

Following the Walker Cup match in 2001, Luke joined the ranks of professional golfers and went on to win his card at the Bear Lakes Country Club to play on the U.S. PGA Tour during the 2002 season and in November he rounded off what had already been a very successful first season as a professional by winning his first tournament, the Southern Farm Bureau Classic at the Annandale Golf Club in Madison, Mississippi. The tournament was curtailed to three rounds by heavy rain, but Luke won with a three round total of 201, 15 under par. That win exempts him from the need to qualify to play on the U.S. Tour for the next two years.

And so this account of the Club's Honorary Membership closes with the youngest and most recent addition to its number having brought distinction to the Club as an outstanding amateur golfer on the threshold of what will surely be an equally successful career as a professional. His continued success and his demeanour on the course make him a worthy international ambassador for the Club.

Chapter Fifteen

Eighty Years of Artisans Golf

FOLLOWING THE suggestion put forward by Major Paulet, the captain of the parent Club, at a meeting of the Committee on 22nd July 1922, an artisans' section of fifteen men was established later that year "... to enable the Artisan inhabitants of Beaconsfield to take up the game of golf ..." The rules of the new Artisans section, or "Society" as it became known, were based on those of the Artisans' section that had been formed at Burnham Beeches ten years earlier and they initially limited the membership to twenty-five and fixed the annual subscription at one guinea. However, its popularity was such that the following year the parent company increased the maximum number to thirty-five and it went on doing so until, by 1936, the maximum number had been raised to fifty and it has remained at that ever since. Originally in addition to the subscribing members, the Club's greenkeepers were automatically entitled to be members. Now all members of the Club's staff can become members.

The rules permitted the Society to elect up to ten (now five) Honorary Members, and the Club's first two professionals, James Jones and Percy Alliss, were so elected, as in due course were Bob Kenyon and Jimmy Adams. Following a change of practice later on, Alex Crombie and Mike Brothers were made vice-presidents of the Society and for many years all past captains of the parent Club have been made vice-presidents of the Society.

The newly formed Society duly became a member of the national Artisans Golfers Association which had been established the year before, largely through the efforts of Billy Gardner who was a founder member of the Flackwell Heath Artisans Golfers Society and who was later awarded the MBE in recognition of his services to artisan golf over many years.

Annual General Meetings

The first Annual General Meeting of the Society for which records exist was the one held on 3rd August 1928 at the Old Rectory in the Old Town – where all subsequent AGMs right up to the war were held, apart from two that were held at the parent clubhouse. The meeting started at 9 p.m., seventeen members were present and it was chaired by Lt. Colonel Weddell, who had just become the secretary of the parent Club on the resignation of Major Sarel. The secretary of the parent Club has always been the chairman of the Society and later it became traditional for the president of the parent Club to be the president of the Society as well.

The Officers and Committee at this 1928 meeting are recorded as being:

President	Lt. Colonel Du Pre
Chairman	Lt. Colonel R. C. Weddell
Hon. Secretary	E.C. Huggett
Treasurer	A. Tidy
Captain	W. J. Rolfe
Vice-Captain	A. E. Berry†
Committee Members	A. Coxall†, A. E. Hitchcock, C. Hadden, J. Nicholls

The first business of the meeting was the presentation of prizes won in recent competitions, which included the Cripwell Challenge Cup and the Dale Challenge Cup, won by R. Hare and H. W. Child respectively. They each received a replica of the cup and the runners-up each received a set of knives and forks, and a silver cigarette case that had been presented by the Ladies' section was won by Ted Berry. A letter from Major Sarel was read out thanking the artisans for their generous gift of a pair of binoculars on his retirement as their chairman and, under "Any Other Business", there was discussion regarding "members playing round in shirts and braces and the general feeling was against this; members should either wear pull-overs or jackets".

At the AGM the following year, Arthur Coxall was elected captain and Mr. H. O. Johnston was made a vice-president for "having done so much for the Society from the commencement of its existence". The principal item on the agenda was the Section's poor financial situation and, after much discussion as to various ways of raising funds, it was agreed that another concert should be given in the Burnham Hall and that half of the profit would go to the miners' fund and the other half to the Society's funds "less a £5 donation to the St John's Ambulance (fund for bandages)". It was also agreed to raise money by running sweepstakes on the following year's Grand National and the Derby.

During the 1930s, the Society went from strength to strength; it was well established, it had developed a good fixture list, it was not short of members, it had developed traditions and customs of its own and, as the honorary

---

†Ted Berry, the head greenkeeper, Arthur Coxall, the club steward and James Jones, the club professional, who was also a member of the Society, constituted the artisans Handicap Committee at this time.

secretary (Arthur Coxall) was pleased to announce at the 1936 AGM, the Society was still solvent – there being a bank balance of nearly £5 – and, he added, "complaints from the parent Club were nil, which proved that we are in their good books". Annual dinners came to be held around this time, the one in 1935 being at the Saracen's Head in the Old Town. Professor Dudgham from the parent Club's Committee was invited to take the chair and, according to the Society's records, "the Dinner was a great success and enabled artisans to meet members of the parent Club". The following year, all the directors and members of the parent Club's Committee were invited to the Society's Annual Dinner during which Colonel Du Pre announced that he would donate the prizes for all the artisans' competitions that year.

The Clubhouse

For several years after the Society was formed in 1922, there were no premises on the course for them to use as a changing room; they had to arrive with their clubs ready to play and this continued to be the position for several years. The first reference in surviving records to there being any artisans' club premises is in a minute of the AGM held on 26th January 1934, when the incoming Committee is asked "to deal with the question of improvements being made inside the Artisans Hut". There is no further reference to the "hut" for several years, but it is fairly certain that it was the one known from later records to have been situated in the copse to the right of the current medal tee at the 6th hole.

In the early days, most of the artisan members lived in the Old Town and to get to the course they would have taken the public footpath from Amersham Road to the 5th tee and would have started to play from there or from the 6th or 14th tees. It is probably for that reason that permission had originally been given to erect the hut in the copse near the 6th tee. Maurice Lidgely, who has been an artisan member for over fifty years, well remembers that when, in 1948 at the age of thirteen, his father pressed him into playing golf with the artisans, most of them used to leave their bicycles at his parents' house which was near that footpath on Amersham Road and make their way to the course over the public footpath. He clearly recalls the hut near the 6th tee and that it was not very luxurious – "although it did have a few chairs ranged around a table in the middle and at least it provided somewhere for us to change". An oil lamp provided light.

In July 1951, the artisans' "hut" was relocated in the enclosed ground between the tees at the 2nd hole and the railway bridge that leads to the 13th fairway; it was about fifty yards from the bridge. The Board donated £250 "towards the cost of improving their headquarters" and a generator was installed to provide electricity.

However, it was not long before those premises became "unserviceable" and so when, in 1959, a wooden bungalow in Seer Green became available, with the Board's approval, the artisans bought the bungalow, dismantled it and erected it on the site that it still occupies today.

The question of extending these premises was subsequently discussed several times, but it was not until the occasion of the renewal of their Club Licence in 1980 that it was finally agreed to construct a brick extension at the front of the premises so as to provide a kitchen and improved toilet facilities and to meet building and fire regulations. The work was under-

The opening of the extension to the Artisans Clubhouse in 1981. Left to right: Colin Paterson (president), Maurice Lidgley and Mrs. Paterson

taken by the artisans themselves and, by working on the project from 8 a.m. to midday every Sunday throughout that winter, it was completed in May 1981. Colin Paterson, as president of both clubs, was invited to open this improved facility and a party, complete with a large iced cake, was held to celebrate the occasion. The party started at midday and went on – well, for quite some time.

Starting Times and Subscriptions

Artisans' subscriptions reflect the fact that their hours of play at weekends and on public holidays are restricted. There are no records of the restricted hours of play that originally applied to artisan membership, but the rules of the Society as revised in 1938 provided that there was to be no play between 9.30 a.m. and 5.30 p.m. on Saturdays and Sundays except that during the period from November to February play could start at 2.45 p.m. Those revised rules also re-enforced the basic membership requirements that applicants must live within three miles of the Beaconsfield postal district, have resided there for at least six months and be approved for membership by the parent Club Committee.

The permitted starting times at weekends and public holidays were subsequently modified from time to time and by 1960 had come to be:

January, February, November, December	Before 9 a.m; after 2 p.m.
March & October	Before 9 a.m; after 3 p.m.
April to September	Before 9 a.m; after 5 p.m.

The current starting times are:

Summer

Saturdays (fourballs)	Before 6.30 a.m. (and past 11th by 8.15 a.m.) After 5 pm.
Sundays & Public Holidays (twoballs)	Before 6.30 a.m; after 5 p.m.

Winter

Sundays & Public Holidays (twoballs)	12 noon to 1 p.m.

The original artisans' annual subscription of one guinea remained unchanged until 1933 when, for some undisclosed reason, it was raised by nine shillings, a development which led the artisans to express the hope at their AGM "that this was only a temporary measure". And so it turned out, for the following year the subscription reverted to a guinea.

On the outbreak of war in 1939, the Club Committee took various "wartime measures", including one that allowed artisan members who were called up to have the courtesy of the course during their military service subject, of course, to the usual terms as to permitted hours of play. Any subscriptions that had actually been paid in respect of the period since the date of their call-up were remitted. At the same time, the Committee expressed the hope that, since several of the greenkeeping staff had also been called-up for military service, those artisan members who were above military age or were not engaged on military service for some other reason, would show their appreciation by assisting on the course during the summer months.

Apart from the temporary increase in 1933, the artisans' subscription remained unchanged for twenty-six years and it was not until after the parent Club had become a members' Club in 1948 that the subscription was increased to two guineas in 1949 and to three guineas in 1956.

The subscription rate was again discussed by the parent Club in 1985, when, having reviewed information obtained from neighbouring clubs about artisans' subscriptions and work requirements, the Board suggested that, instead of an increase in subscriptions, the artisans should increase their current work requirement "to include the following in order of priority commitment":

Carrying out divoting to fairways as required.
Carrying out repairs to tees as required.
Raking bunkers thoroughly at weekends during their playing round.
Assisting with furniture moving in the parent clubhouse as required.
Tending gardens surrounding the clubhouse.

However, this proposal did not find much favour with the artisans with the result that the work requirement was not altered and the annual subscription was increased by seventy-five percent as from the following January. Although for a variety of reasons, the artisans were not disposed on that occasion to accept additional work requirements as an alternative to a subscription increase, on many subsequent occasions the artisans have continued to contribute to the maintenance and upkeep of the course beyond just "divoting". For example, in liaison with the head greenkeeper, they have periodically undertaken clearing activities in wooded areas and, during the reconstruction of the 15th green and the extensive turf laying activity associated with the bunker renovation programme in the mid-1990s, the artisans voluntarily afforded considerable help to the greenstaff.

Trophies and Matches

As mentioned earlier, the Cripwell and Dale Challenge Cups were among the earliest of the artisans' twenty-three named trophies for which they currently play. Another is the Challenge Cup which was presented to the artisans by the Ladies' section in 1931. In 1965, Vesey Raffety, the President of the two clubs, donated a bronze model of a golfer as the trophy for the Artisans Club Championship that was instituted that year.

A trophy with an unusual background is the one presented to the Artisans Club by a Dennis Hawkins who had at one time been a very active artisan golfer in the Bournemouth area, but who eventually went to live in the United States. Apparently he was so impressed when he read in an artisans' golf journal of the amount of money raised for charity by the Beaconsfield artisans that, in 1985, he presented them with a suitably inscribed plaque which is played for annually in the Denis Hawkins Scramble.

One of the best of the artisan golfers was Eddie Bovingdon whose name appears many times on the various honours boards in their clubhouse. Perhaps his most successful season was in 1955 when he won the Vice-Presidents Cup, the Schweppes Trophy, the Montrose Cloete Cup, the Cripwell Cup, the Du Pre Cup, the Ladies' cup and (jointly with Ted Lidgley) the Lifeboat Spoons. He became a scratch golfer in 1962.

Friendly home and away matches have been played for several years against the artisans of other local clubs such as Ashridge, Banstead Downs, Coulsdon Court and Temple. In the early 1960s, matches were also arranged with St Georges Hill and Hadley Wood and, more recently, a annual away match against Piltdown has been played each October.

Some twenty years ago, the Thames Valley League was established comprising the artisans clubs of Beaconsfield, Denham, Flackwell Heath, Gerrards Cross, Harewood Downs and Maidenhead. When asked how

Beaconsfield fares in the League, a somewhat non-committal response is given: "We have not done so well lately." Notwithstanding the results, these League matches are among the highlights of the Club's year.

No account of the artisans' matches would be complete without mention of their fixtures during each May public holiday weekend against the artisans of some of the leading clubs in the Lancashire/Cheshire area. These fixtures, which are on a home and away basis in alternate years, started in 1988 with a match against the Southport & Ainsdale artisans, but they now include matches against Birkdale, Formby, West Lancs and Wallasey. Information from usually reliable sources suggests that an away tour of these clubs is not just a golfing experience !

Joe Lawrence – British Artisans Golf Champion 1960

Over the years, there have been several members of the Artisans Club such as Ted Berry, Eddie Bovingden, Ernie Leslie and Bryan Payne who have had handicaps of scratch or near scratch and who have won many trophies and achieved representative honours. Bryan Payne, for example, was a member of the Artisans Club for some thirty years and, in addition to winning many trophies, played in the BB&O artisans county team on several occasions. He also played for the England artisans team in an international match at Moor Park.

There is, however, little doubt that Joe Lawrence was the best artisan golfer at Beaconsfield. In the 1930s, Joe was an assistant to Percy Allis when he was the professional at Beaconsfield and he claimed to have made Peter Alliss his first cut-down golf clubs – that would have been when Peter was about five or six years old. However, Joe gave up the idea of professional golf as a career and, after the war, became a film cameraman at Pinewood and joined the Artisans Club around 1948. He subsequently won the BB&O Artisans' Championship no less than eight times and was once runner-up in the Evening News Golf Tournament played at Camberley Heath. What was unquestionably his greatest success came on 27th July 1960, when he won the British Artisans Golf Championship at Moor Park. The next year, Joe broke the amateur course record at Beaconsfield with a 68, which, playing off a handicap of plus 2, gave him a net 70 in the competition. In later years, Joe moved to Stoke Poges (as it then was) where his name appears on several honours boards.

Interestingly, Joe's daughter married Jim Hume who, in 1959, had come from Gullane to be assistant professional to Alex Crombie at Beaconsfield. Jim left Beaconsfield after only eighteen months when he was offered the post of professional at Harewood Downs where he stayed for five years. He and his wife have since returned to Gullane where he is still the professional.

178

It was while Jimmy was at Harewood Downs that, on one occasion, he and Joe Lawrence partnered each other in the Wentworth Foursomes and created a considerable sensation in the national sports press by defeating the much fancied pairing of Ted Dexter, the England cricket captain, and Arthur Lees, a former Ryder Cup player, at the 18th – having been three down with eight to play.

Some Notable Artisan Members

It is always invidious to select for particular mention some individuals and not others from within any group of people – especially when that group is as small and closely knit as is the Artisans Club. Nevertheless,

Joe Lawrence, British Artisan champion, 1960

there have been some artisan members who deserve particular mention because of their significant contribution in one way or another to the well-being and functioning of their club. With the help and agreement of the Artisans' Committee, it is felt that the following artisans are particularly worthy of mention.

TED LIDGLEY

Ted Lidgely played in the Artisan Cup competition in 1934 and he was probably a member of the Artisans Club even earlier. Throughout his membership, Ted worked tirelessly for the Club of which he was always proud to be a member. Except for 1946, Ted was captain continuously from 1939 to 1952 and it was while he was again captain in 1958 that, sadly, he became seriously ill and died on 26th July that year. It is in his memory that the Lidgley Shield is played for annually by the two clubs.

ARTHUR TAPPING

Arthur joined the Artisans Club in 1936 and for fifty years devoted much of his time to the welfare and development of the Club. He was elected captain in 1957 and, in 1986, to mark his half century of membership, he was made a Life Member. Sadly, and yet after so many years devotion to golf, perhaps fittingly, Arthur died on the 15th tee in 1996. A memorial bench has been placed at that tee.

ROGER BISHOP

Although not a great golfer, Roger was a very popular member and the mainstay of the Club during the 1950s and 1960s. He was its honorary secretary for eighteen years from 1968 and on his retirement from that position in 1986 he was made a Life Member at the suggestion of Colin Paterson who was the then president of the two clubs.

179

The Berry Brothers. Left to right: Tom, Ted (the head greenkeeper for many years) and Bill

MAURICE LIDGLEY

Maurice "joined" the Artisans Club or, as he puts it, he was made by his father to play golf with the artisans, in 1948 and eventually attained a handicap of 9. No member of the Artisans Club, save perhaps his father, has worked harder and for longer to keep the Club going and its continued existence owes much to his dedication. Maurice has been a member for over fifty years and was elected captain in 1962 and again in 1980.

TED BERRY

Ted was one of three brothers who were all members of the Artisans Club at least by 1928. Ted and his brother Bill were both present at the Club's first AGM for which records exist and on that occasion they received 5s. and 10s. vouchers for coming fourth and second respectively in the *News of the World* club competition. Ted was head greenkeeper for more than twenty-five years and was one of the Club's longest serving members; he was elected captain in 1934 and again in 1954 and 1955. He was a very good golfer who is recorded as having a handicap of plus 4 at one stage. The other brother Tom, the father of Andrew Berry, who has been a member of the parent Club since 1960, was also a good golfer.

It should be recorded that the current efficient and enthusiastic artisans' honorary secretary, Steve Reed, has himself been a member of the Artisans' Club since 1980 and secretary for the last eleven years. In 1991, together with the parent club captain, Hamish Paton, and secretary, Ivor Anderson, he was involved in the redrafting of the artisans' rules and the change of its name from "Society" to "Club". Similarly, the current treasurer, Roy Wilkinson, is a long-standing member and has held office as treasurer since 1992.

The Artisans Club's officers in 2002. Left to right: Peter Strawa (captain),
Steve Reed (honorary secretary), and Roy Wilkinson (honorary treasurer)

Two Clubs over Eighty Years

It was the Artisans Club's seventy-fifth anniversary in 1997 and the occasion
was marked by appropriate events during the year. The celebrations
culminated on 6th September in an eighteen hole sponsored competition
with over a hundred members and their guests from neighbouring clubs
taking part. At the Gala Dinner at the parent clubhouse that followed the
competition, the parent club's captain, Jim Lawson, presented the artisans
captain, Barry Kitching, with a cheque with which to buy new tables for their
clubroom.

In the Programme for the event and in the speeches at the Dinner that
followed, many references were made to the close and co-operative
relationship that has existed between the two clubs from the very beginning
and nowhere is that relationship more manifest each year than in the long-
standing golfing fixtures between the two clubs.

Records of the parent Club include references to the playing of foursome
medal competitions for the Artisan's Cup in the 1930s. The earliest record is
dated 30th June 1934 when the winners were Mr. B. W. Willett and Mr.
A. H. Child of the parent and artisan Clubs respectively with a score of 82
gross, net 70. The next record relates to the competition played on 27th June
1936, when Ted Lidgley, Ted Berry, the head greenkeeper, Arthur Tidy and

WITH THE CLUBS

BEACONSFIELD.—Monthly Stableford: K. V. Braddon, 41 points, A. H. Gold 36 points. Artisans' Cup, Greensome Stableford: H. C. Staines and E. Lidgley (21) won on the last nine holes after a tie with R. C. Brown and A. Tapping (19) at 35 points. The latter couple were second on the last six holes after a tie with three other pairs.

Extract from Golf Illustrated, *July 1951*

Arthur Coxall, the parent Club's steward, were among the artisans who took part. Records do not show when the format of this competition was changed but, as the report of the competition in the *Golf Illustrated* magazine shows, by 1951 the Artisans Cup had become a greensome stableford as opposed to a foursome medal. That year, the winners were Harold Staines and Ted Lidgley on the last nine holes after a tie on 35 points with R.C. Brown and Arthur Tapping.

By 1955 the Artisan Cup had become a fourball competition and a new competition, the Coronation Foursomes, had come into the fixture list. Again, the pairings for this new competition consisted of a parent and an artisan Club member.

In addition to these competitions, there were also annual team matches between the two clubs on a rotating annual home and away basis and, while the joint competitions have now ceased to be played because of crowded fixture lists, the team matches continue as The Club v. The Artisans and The President's Team v. The Artisans. The former of these is the keenly contested match for the Lidgley Shield which was purchased in 1960 from contributions made by members of both clubs in memory of Ted Lidgley.

Similarly, for many years there have also been two fixtures a year between the artisans and the Ladies' section and these are on the same rotating home and away basis. The format of these fixtures has changed over the years from matches to foursome Stableford competitions; today, both the spring and autumn fixtures are greensome Stableford competitions in which each pairing consists of a lady member and an artisan.

While there are many people today who regard the artisan sections of golf clubs as anachronisms, for eighty years now there has been a valued and special relationship between the two clubs at Beaconsfield, confirmed by the continued participation in inter-club matches and functions. It is a relationship that endures to the benefit of both clubs.

Chapter Sixteen

The Centenary and Beyond

AND SO A hundred years of golf at Beaconsfield draw to their close. There have been many, many changes in that time both within the Club and in golf generally, but it is probably true to say that, given those changes, Colonel Du Pre would have been as proud today of the Club that he founded as he was when he was alive.

The centenary celebrations have also come and gone and have been thoroughly enjoyed by members and their guests. The task of organizing the social events of the centenary year rested of course with the Social Committee whose members, Rob Lucas, chairman, Janet Gore and Barbara Mackin worked extremely hard throughout the year, and they and their many volunteer helpers fully deserved the success that they achieved. In addition to the usual events in the Club's social calendar, there were several centenary functions to organize of which the two principal ones were the Centenary Summer Ball and the "Family Fun Day". The Centenary Summer Ball was held on Saturday 8th June, when more than 250 members and guests enjoyed a champagne reception followed by dining and dancing until the early hours of the morning in a marquee resplendently decorated by helpers from the Ladies' section with flowers and ribbons predominantly in the Club's colours. The Members' Bar, though perhaps less resplendent in its garb, was given over to a disco which, despite certain initial misgivings on the part of the Social Committee, proved to be an enormous success.

The social celebrations concluded with the August Family Fun Day when over 300 members, guests, children, grandchildren and even great-grandchildren enjoyed the barbecue and all the fun of the fair at the stalls and the round-abouts and then tried their skill in the putting, chipping and other competitions. The fact that the sun shone brightly on all this revelry on an August day in England only reflects the military thoroughness with which the whole event had been prepared.

After the several successful Pro-Ams that had been held in the past, it was altogether fitting that the golfing events of the centenary year should have culminated in another highly successful Pro-Am competition in July. It was a just reward for the considerable efforts of the organizing committee and its army of helpers that the event produced a record entry, that a new professional course record was created, and that two members of the Club, one lady and one man, were in the winning team. The sun shone, a festive atmosphere pervaded the clubhouse and there was great enjoyment for all those who took part.

There were many individual golfing achievements during the year and several of them have already been mentioned in other chapters. One achievement, however, that is not mentioned elsewhere lies not so much in success in a single event, but rather in a consistency that seems to be reserved only for the good players. In the decade or so since he became a member of the Club, Tim Whittaker has been one of the Club's best and most consistent players and he well demonstrated that during the centenary year. In Club competitons, he was runner-up in the Club Championship, which he had won on three previous occasions, he won the Scratch Knock-out Cup as well as the newly instituted Scratch Order of Merit. Outside the Club, he was runner-up in the County Championship, which was played at Beaconsfield this year, and he qualified to play in the final Qualifying Rounds for the Open which were played at Gullane and where, although he did not eventually qualify to play in the Open, he returned the very commendable 36 hole score of 144 (73 + 71). A very fine centenary year achievement.

During the centenary year, the Juniors section has continued to develop under their organiser, Walter Gutteridge, and his assistants Geoff Bradshaw, Jack Campbell, Bernie Carroll, Tim Clutterbuck, Ian Warren and Hilda Wright. Another member of the Club, Barbara Pratt, has been the County Juniors organiser during the centenary year and she will be succeeded in that role by Hilda Wright. The Club's considerable commitment to junior golf bodes well for its future.

To bring the Club's successful centenary golfing season to a fitting close, the Scratch League team, under the captaincy of the centenary year club champion, Richard Clarke, recorded a home victory in September over Stoke Poges Golf Club to ensure that they remain in Division One for another year and Luke Donald won his first professional tournament.

After what he describes as a "steady season", but which by any standard has been a remarkably successful first season as a professional, our own man in America, Luke Donald, seems certain, at the time of going to print, to retain his "card" for next year's season on the USPGA Tour. His continued success and his continued demeanour on the course make him a worthy overseas ambassador for the Club.

Before leaving the centenary year's achievements in the golf related field, it is appropriate and pleasing to record that for the first time in the Club's history, one of its members, Tim Clutterbuck, has become president-elect of the Berks, Bucks & Oxon Union of Golf Clubs. Tim, who has represented the Club's interests on the BB&O Executive Committee for several years, will take office in March next year and the good wishes of all members go to him for a successful and enjoyable term in office. Tim also carries with him the distinction of having been the last Club member to have beaten Luke Donald playing level.

Richard Clarke, centenary year club champion and captain of the First Team

Against the background of all this fine golf and all the fun and excitement of the year's events, it is difficult to visualize what it must have been like when golf at Beaconsfield first started a hundred years ago with the inspiration and enthusiasm of one man, a nine hole course, a few golfing friends and a shed just off Potkiln Lane. And it is equally difficult for us to visualize what golf at Beaconsfield may be like after another hundred years. Will there still be Mid-week Medals in 2102? Will Thursday still be Ladies' Day at Beaconsfield? Will men be allowed to wear calf length or even ankle length socks? Will the Wildebeests still be playing Henley for the Basil Evans Cup and will the Scratch League team still be in Division One? It is stimulating to ask such questions parochial as they may be and to postulate answers, but they only serve to show just how our vision of the future is necessarily constrained by our present knowledge such that it becomes impossible even to formulate intelligent questions as to the distant future. In any case, it is not good to dwell too long on such idle speculations lest our love of the present and the traditions of the past set us too much against the inevitability of evolution and change.

But there are some matters of the present that cast shadows of uncertainty and possible change over the more immediate future.

There is, for example, the long-standing suggestion relating to the so-called Wilton Park diversion which, if it were to be adopted and follow one of the alternative routes that have been proposed, would cut across the 4th, 5th and 6th holes, would pass close to Golf Cottage and would be likely to lead to in-filling housing development between the bypass and the

Amersham Road (A 355). Happily, current opinion seems to be that the final report of the traffic consultants engaged by the local traffic authorities will not include a proposal for such a bypass.

And then there is the proposal of the Central Railway consortium for an express freightlink from the north-west through the Chilterns to the Channel Tunnel and beyond. This proposal, if approved, would eventually involve, so it is said, long, high-speed freight trains traveling on the track through the course and Seer Green station every fifteen minutes or so in each direction. There are many who question the economic viability of that whole proposal, but since it is a proposal that clearly involves aspects of the central government's transport policy, in relation to road and rail usage, the outcome of the House of Commons decision on the matter cannot yet be predicted. It would be ironic, indeed, if the very railway line that brought life and prosperity to the Club in the first place were to become the source of major interference with its present amenities.

Then there is the future of Wilton Park itself, for it is common knowledge that within the next several years, the military authorities are likely to vacate those premises. Inevitably, there is uncertainty as to what use of that land may be permitted in that eventuality.

These clouds, though of concern, do not threaten the existence of the Club and, given its sound and stable financial position, its continually improving course, its flourishing Juniors section and its standing in the golfing community, its future as a traditional private members' Club has never been more assured. Undoubtedly, the Club will continue to evolve and that evolution will inevitably bring change, but hopefully a knowledge of its history and its traditions will prove a helpful guide to those involved in that process.

Appendix One

PRESIDENTS

1948	Sir Alexander R. Murray KCIE, CBE
1950	L. Padfield MC
1958	E. Whitley-Jones
1963	C. V. Raffety
1970	R. C. Edwards
1975	H. C. Staines
1980	C. W. Paterson MC
1985	A. M. Hamilton
1991	B. C. Hines
1996	D. G. Randall
2001	His Honour Judge R. D. Connor

CAPTAINS

1948	A. R. Wylie	1967	C. T. C. Woodall MBE, TD	1986	W. M. Houston
1949	W. T. Birch	1968	K. V. Braddon	1987	M. A. Wisdom
1950	G. I. Price	1969	D. B. Wilson	1988	Air Vice-Marshall K. Kingshott CBE, DFC
1951	S. J. C. Weedon	1970	Dr. A. S. McLean		
1952	A. P. Case	1971	J. R. Adair	1989	R. F. H. Crabb
1953	W. L. Robertson	1972	C. W. Paterson, MC	1990	W. P. C. Horgan
1954	C. V. Raffety	1973	A. M. Hamilton	1991	H. K. Paton
1955	H. F. Randall	1974	J. T. A. May	1992	A. Berry
1956	W. R. F. Bennett	1975	D. G. Randall	1993	D. C. Abbott
1957	H. C. Staines	1976	R. G. F. Chase	1994	D. Lewis
1958	A. W. H. Baucher	1977	A. N. W. Neale	1995	G. W. Bull
1959	D. K. Gordon	1978	J. C. Woods	1996	J. Lawson
1960	Lt. Col. E. B. N. Taylor	1979	J. D. Mortimer DFC	1997	G. C. Tuck
1961	C. H. Crockwell	1980	G. R. Irving	1998	K. M. Robertson
1962	E. E. Monk	1981	L. S. F. Charles	1999	A. J. Robertson
1963	R. C. Edwards	1982	R. F. L. Zeidler	2000	J. R. Sutton
1964	W. Davidson	1983	B. C. Hines	2001	C. Biffa
1965	E. Hodges	1984	C. Smith	2002	D. J. Brown
1966	F. P. Whaley	1985	R. D. Connor		

LADIES CAPTAINS

1948 Miss M. R. Greaves	1967 Mrs. W. L. Robertson	1986 Mrs. R. A. Clough
1949 Miss M. R. Greaves	1968 Mrs. D. Ellis	1987 Mrs. M. D. Lee
1950 Miss J. MacFarlane	1969 Mrs. H. C. Brown	1988 Mrs. J. J. Burton
1951 Mrs. J. W. Paul	1970 Mrs. H. A. Thomas	1989 Mrs. A. St Bayley
1952 Mrs. J. W. Paul	1971 Mrs. R. G. F. Chase	1990 Mrs. P. A. F. Wisdom
1953 Mrs. R. G. H. Salmon	1972 Mrs. D. O. MacDougall	1991 Mrs. C. Cooke
1954 Mrs. A. W. Baucher	1973 Mrs. G. V. Maund	1992 Mrs. J. Taylor
1955 Mrs. E. Whitley-Jones	1974 Mrs. D. J. W. Anthony	1993 Mrs. J. P. Wright
1956 Mrs. E. Whitley-Jones	1975 Mrs. E. R. Gillespie	1994 Mrs. N. A. Croft
1957 Mrs. R. A. K. Wiener	1976 Mrs. D. S. McIntosh	1995 Mrs. V.L. Thackrah
1958 Lady Masson	1977 Mrs. I. H. P. Laughland	Hinde
1959 Mrs. W. S. Foley	1978 Mrs. J. L. Mawhood	1996 Mrs. J. E. A. Goodwyn
1960 Mrs. H. B. S. Benson	1979 Mrs. G. A. Elliot	1997 Mrs. J. A. Lucas
1961 Mrs. R. Burgess	1980 Mrs. W. Rademaker	1998 Mrs. M. A. Horgan
1962 Mrs. G. I. Price	1981 Mrs. J. M. Chapman	1999 Mrs. S. G. Crabb
1963 Mrs. C. D. Eberstein	1982 Mrs. A. K. Berry	2000 Mrs. A. S. Pegley 2001
1964 Mrs. W. Davidson	1983 Mrs. B. Rigby	2001 Mrs. J. A. Gill
1965 Mrs. C. V. Raffety	1984 Mrs. C. R. Green	2002 Mrs. S. J. Edwards
1966 Mrs. J. M. Grove	1985 Mrs. K. M. Bartlett	

SECRETARIES

1948	Lt. Col. H. Sutherland
1951	Lt. Col. H. "Gunga" Dean OBE, MC
1964	C. Crockwell†
1969	Lt. Commander Franklin
1970	S. J. A. MacDonald
1973	Major J. R. Adair†
1974	W. R. Pluck
1979	J. Anderson†
1979	M. J. R. Hunter
1987	Air Vice-Marshall K. Kingshott CBE, DFC†
1987	J. K. A. O'Brien
1988	P. I. Anderson
1996	R. E. Thomas
2001	K. R. Wilcox

†Charles Crockwell, Jimmy Adair, John Anderson and Ken Kingshott were members of the Club who, in the particular circumstances of their times, acted as secretary on an interim basis.

LIFE MEMBERS	HONORARY MEMBERS
J. R. Adair A. M. Hamilton B. C. Hines	P. Alliss M. Brothers
Mrs. M. R. Price Mrs. C. Watson	L. C. Donald

Appendix Two

CLUB CHAMPIONS

1948	K. V. Braddon	1966	R. G. Ling	1985	D. Lewis
1949	K. V. Braddon	1967	R. V. Braddon	1986	M. J. Fennell
1950	W. L. Robertson	1968	R. V. Braddon	1987	A. J. Bobath
1951	I. R. Harris	1969	H. C. E. Maynard	1988	I. D. Wheater
1952	W. L. Robertson	1970	R. V. Braddon	1989	T. J. E. Clough
1953	I. R. Harris	1971	R. V. Braddon	1990	T. C. Whittaker
1954	W. L. Robertson	1972	I. D. Wheater	1991	B. Muir
1955	J. W. Chance	1973	I. D. Wheater	1992	L. C. Donald
1956	W. W. Monk	1974	I. D. Wheater	1993	G. E. Barnes
1957	W. L. Robertson	1976	I. D. Wheater	1994	L. C. Donald
1958	W. L. Robertson	1977	I. D. Wheater	1995	T. C. Whittaker
1959	W. L. Robertson	1978	I. D. Wheater	1996	D. J. Batten
1960	R. V. Braddon	1979	I. D. Wheater	1997	T. C. Whittaker
1961	R. G. Ling	1980	I. D. Wheater	1998	P. G. Neal
1962	R. V. Braddon	1981	I. D. Wheater	1999	G. N. Franklin
1963	C. T. C. Woodall	1982	F. George	2000	P. G. Neal
1964	P. K. Entwistle	1983	I. D. Wheater	2001	R. Christian
1965	R. G. Ling	1984	D. A. McCay	2002	R. J. Clarke

LADIES CLUB CHAMPIONS

1951	Mrs. A. H. Gold	1979	Miss J. Warren	1992	Mrs. C. Watson
1952	Mrs. J. W. Paul	1980	Miss J. Warren	1993	Mrs. C. Watson
1953	Mrs. R. G. H. Salmon	1981	Mrs. A. Laughland	1994	Mrs. C. Watson
1954	Mrs. A. W. Baucher	1982	Miss J. Warren	1995	Mrs. C. Watson
1955	Mrs. K. V. Braddon	1983	Mrs. I. H. P. Laughland	1996	Mrs. C. Watson
1956	Mrs. A. W. Baucher	1984	Miss J. Warren	1997	Mrs. C. Watson
1957	Mrs. A. W. Baucher	1985	Mrs. L. Wheater	1998	Mrs. C. Watson
	[Not played]	1986	Miss J. Warren	1999	Mrs. C. Watson
1974	Mrs. I. H. P. Laughland	1987	Mrs. C. Watson	2000	Mrs. C. Watson
1975	Mrs. W. E. Bartlett	1988	Mrs. C. Watson	2001	Mrs. C. Watson
1976	Mrs. W. E. Bartlett	1989	Mrs. C. Watson	2002	Mrs. C. Watson
1977	Mrs. I. H. P. Laughland	1990	Mrs. C. Watson		
1978	Mrs. I. H. P. Laughland	1991	Mrs. C. Watson		

JUNIORS CHAMPIONS

1990	M. Chagouri	1995	P. G. Neal	2000	T. Platt
1991	S. D. Harris	1996	P. G. Neal	2001	T. Platt
1992	L. C. Donald	1997	P. G. Neal	2002	M. C. Drummond
1993	L. C. Donald	1998	P. G. Neal		
1994	L. C. Donald	1999	R. J. Clarke		

Appendix Three

LUKE DONALD

Principal Achievements as an Amateur

1992 & 1994	Beaconsfield Club Champion
1993	BB&O Boys Champion
1995	South of England Champion
1996 & 1997	BB&O Amateur champion
1996	Midland Amateur champion
	Winner of The Berkhamsted Trophy
1997	Winner of the Lagonda Trophy
1998	Member of English team in the Home Internationals
	Eisenhower Trophy (GB&I team): 3rd Individual
1999	Led Qualifiers at Panmure for The Open at Muirfield
	Member of winning GB&I Walker Cup team at Nairn and won all four of his own matches
1998-2000	While at North Western University, USA, Luke received many awards including in 1999 the Jack Nicklaus Award for the outstanding Collegiate Player of the year. He won thirteen College Tournaments including the Kepler, Fossum, Aldila and Dr. Pepper Intercollegiates, the Widon Memorial and the NCAA Individual Championship. In the 1999 season he achieved a Low Stroke Average in College Tournaments of 70.45 – beating the previous record of 70.61 held by Tiger Woods.
2000	Winner of the North-East Amateur Championship [USA]
	US Amateur Championship semi-finalist
	Winner of the Chicago Open [Being an amateur, Luke was not able to accept the winner's prize money.]
2001	Member of winning GB&I Walker Cup team at Sea Island (USA) and won three of his own matches.
	Became a Professional Golfer
2002	Winner of the Southern Farm Bureau Classic on the US PGA tour